CULTURES OF THE WORLD®

GERMANY

Barbara Fuller/Gabriele Vossmeyer

BENCHMARK BOOKS

MARSHALL CAVENDISH
NEW YORK

PICTURE CREDITS
Cover photo: © Art Directors & TRIP/Adina Tovy
AFP: 37, 59, 100, 111 • Allgemeiner Deutscher: 25, 34, 49, 51, 67, 74, 79, 80, 81, 84, 86, 90, 101, 105, 115 • Art Directors & TRIP: 55, 57, 58, 60, 61, 117 • Bes Stock: 19, 116 • Bundesarchiv: 29 • Victor Englebert: 85, 109, 110 • Focus Team: 1, 14, 38, 46, 52, 54, 64, 68, 78, 93, 126 • The Image Bank: 9, 10, 11, 13, 16, 17, 18, 20, 21, 23, 35, 43, 44, 45, 47, 48, 50, 53, 63, 66, 69, 71, 73, 83, 89, 97, 103, 113, 118, 119, 127 • Life File Photographic Library: 15, 24, 76, 125, 129 • Sachsische Landesbibliothek: 26, 27, 28, 31 • Lonely Planet Images: 30 • David Simson: 77 • Topham Picturepoint: 112 • Gabriele Vossmeyer: 3, 4, 5, 6, 7, 8, 12, 22, 36, 39, 40, 42, 56, 62, 65, 70, 72, 75, 82, 88, 95, 96, 99, 106, 107, 108, 121, 122, 123, 124, 128, 130, 131

ACKNOWLEDGMENTS
With thanks to Ms. Suzanne Santos for her expert reading of this manuscript

PRECEDING PAGE
A musical group in traditional dress performs at the English Garden in Munich.

Marshall Cavendish Corporation
99 White Plains Road
Tarrytown, NY 10591
Website: www.marshallcavendish.com

Originated and designed by
Times Books International, an imprint of
Times Media Private Limited, a member of
Times International Publishing

Printed in Malaysia

Library of Congress Cataloging-in-Publication Data
Fuller, Barbara, 1961-
Germany / by Barbara Fuller and Gabriele Vossmeyer.— 2nd ed.
    p. cm. — (Cultures of the world)
Summary: Explores the geography, history, government, economy, people and culture of Germany.
Includes bibliographical references and index.
    ISBN 0-7614-1667-6
1. Germany—Juvenile literature. [1. Germany.] I. Vossmeyer, Gabriele. II. Title. III. Series: Cultures of the world (2nd ed.).
DD17.F85 2003
943—dc21   2003008186

7 6 5 4 3

CONTENTS

This charming square in Cologne is decorated with colorful flower beds and sculptures.

The impressive Great St. Martin church in Cologne was built in the Gothic style.

INTRODUCTION

THE FEDERAL REPUBLIC OF GERMANY sits in the center of Europe, surrounded by nine other European nations. Germany's rich culture has been influential in the development of Western arts and philosophy. Beethoven, Goethe, Nietzsche, Marx, and Einstein, to name but a few, have influenced generations of musicians, writers, philosophers, politicians, and scientists worldwide.

Although the Third Reich and World War II brought Germany almost to the point of total destruction, Germans swiftly brought their country back on its feet through hard work and determination, yielding years of prosperity. The reunification of Germany, formalized in October 1990 after 45 years of separation, affects every aspect of life in the country, from law enforcement to working conditions, and from housing to funding of the arts and sports.

Despite some economic problems in recent years, Germany is still regarded as the "economic engine" of the European Union and, as such, Germany is expected to continue to play a major role in both European and world affairs.

GEOGRAPHY

THE ALPS ARE GERMANY'S most prominent geographical feature. Unlike other mountain ranges in the world, the Alps do not form an unbroken chain; instead, the range is divided by many deep valleys.

Scientists believe that during the last ice age, about 18,000 years ago, glaciers from Scandinavia and northern Europe advanced onto central Europe and covered the entire European continent, including the Alps. As the glaciers melted away, they left distinctive marks across Europe's terrain.

The force of the glaciers' retreat widened the gaps between the mountains in the Alps. This created numerous U-shaped valleys. Deep, enclosed valleys were filled with water, creating elongated lakes, such as Lake Constance. Melting water from the mountaintops poured forth to the valleys below, creating enormous waterfalls. The retreating glaciers also carried huge amounts of gravel and debris, which were eventually deposited into the valleys as the glaciers melted away.

The physical features acquired by the Alps during the last ice age have given the Alpine terrain its characteristic unevenness. Thus, the Alps divide Germany into three distinct regions: the North German Lowlands, the Central Highlands, and the Alps and the Alpine Foreland.

The geological characteristics of each region actually cover an area farther east and west than Germany's current borders. The Lowlands, for example, stretch west into the Netherlands and Belgium and east through Poland's Silesian plain to as far as the Ural Mountains in Russia. The Oder River and Neisse River provide a natural border with Poland, the Alps provide a natural barrier with Switzerland and Austria, and the Rhine River in the south and southwest forms a natural border with France.

Above: **Sheep graze on a Bavarian farm.**

Opposite: **A farming town along the Rhine River.**

NORTH GERMAN LOWLANDS

The North Sea coast is Germany's most important shipping outlet. The land along the coast is extremely flat and shallow, close to sea level. Dikes have, therefore, been built to protect the land from floods.

Several islands are located off the north coast, including the East Frisian Islands and Helgoland. The latter was formerly used as a naval base but it has now become a haven for the study of birds. Hamburg on the Elbe River and Bremerhaven on the Weser River are major ports. Smaller ports like Wilhelmshaven and Emden on the northwestern tip are also important.

The Baltic coast is a mixture of flat sandy shores and steep cliffs, with shallow natural inlets for ports. In the northernmost part of the country, the Nord-Ostsee Canal links the Baltic to the North Sea.

South of the Baltic Sea, a fertile belt runs from Holstein to Mecklenburg. Brandenburg's low lying plains alternate with wide marshy valleys.

The marshland near the mouth of the Elbe is fertile, but further inland it becomes sandy, with boulders, heath, peat bogs, fens, and marshes. This infertile plain includes two major cities, Hannover and Brunswick.

A vineyard in the Rhine valley.

CENTRAL HIGHLANDS

The Central Highlands is a complex region that consists of a great variety of geographical features—high plains, undulating hills, mountain ranges, and wide river courses.

Germany's largest slate mountains—the Rhineland Schiefergebirge—run across the northwestern part of the country and are bisected by the Rhine River. These mountains in turn are made up of the Eifel Range of 50 cone-shaped extinct volcanoes; the exposed stony plateau of the Hunsrück region; the agricultural areas of Sauerland and Bergischerland; the Rothaargebirge Range; the forested area known as Westerwald; and the heavily wooded Taunus region.

The Ruhr industrial area, where natural iron ore and hard coal deposits have led to the development of huge steel industries, lies to the east of the Rhine and north of the Schiefergebirge.

East of the Rhineland lies the Hesse Central Upland, which includes the Vogelsberg Range. To the north of these mountains is the Harz Range, source of several rivers, such as the Oder, and the site of numerous reservoirs. The east and south slopes of the Harz descend into the Thuringian Basin, an extremely fertile region. Here, grains, such as wheat and barley, and root crops are grown in the flat areas. Orchards and vineyards are found on slopes overlooking the Ilm River.

The Erzgebirge Range, found south of the Thuringian Basin, forms a natural border with the Czech Republic. The range is known as the Ore Mountains, after the silver and tin mines found here in the sixteenth century that were exploited until recent years. The city of Dresden sits on the plain beneath these mountains.

Unusual sandstone rock formations stand in the Elbe Valley near Dresden.

The breathtaking Titisee, or Lake Titi, in the Black Forest was created by glaciers.

THE SOUTHERN HIGHLANDS South of the Schiefergebirge lies the wide Rhine flood plain. The plain enjoys a mild climate, making it extremely fertile. Fruit orchards are planted on the western hills from Frankfurt to Heidelberg. The nearby Neckar Valley, on the other hand, has areas devoted to agriculture and industry. Two of the world's most famous forests lie to the south of the Central Uplands—the Black Forest in the southwest and the Bavarian Forest in the southeast. The Black Forest, named after its numerous dark fir trees, is the source of the Danube and Neckar rivers. The Bavarian Forest is mainly covered with coniferous trees. The national park located here is the largest of its kind in Central Europe.

ALPS AND PRE-ALPS

The Danube, rising in the Black Forest and leaving Germany at Passau in the east on its way to the Black Sea, runs along the northern edge of the Alpine foreland, which rises to an average height of 1,640 feet (5,412 m). Popular lakes such as the Chiemsee, Starnbergersee, and Ammersee are found in this area.

In the northern part of the region, Lower Bavaria's fertile soil is ideal for the production of hops, which are grown for the breweries in nearby Munich. Small marshes, where the water table is high, are also found here. The southern part of the region is higher and wetter, suitable for raising cattle. Augsburg and Munich are the main population centers of the region.

Snow-covered fir trees stand on the slopes of the German Alps.

In the southwest, Lake Constance, 37 miles (59.3 km) long and 9 miles (14.5 km) wide, is nestled in the depression of Alpine fallout moraines (an irregular mass of boulders and gravel). Together with the Chiemsee, Lake Constance makes up part of the Alpine lakes, the focus of considerable settlement, a booming tourism industry, and institutions devoted to scientific studies.

The German Alps are found to the east of Lake Constance and at the border with Austria. From west to east, they are divided into the Allgäu, the Bavarian, and the Berchtesgaden Alps. The north-facing Alpine slopes are forested, and farms with pasture lands dot the south-facing slopes. The lower slopes have mixed forests; conifers lie between 3,000 and 5,600 feet (914 and 1,707 m). Year-round snow is present at over 8,500 feet (2,591 m). The Zugspitze, at 9,725 feet (2,964 m), is Germany's highest mountain. Nearby Garmisch-Partenkirchen is Germany's major ski resort.

Cyclists ride along the overflowing banks of the Rhine River in Cologne.

THE RHINE

The Rhine River is 865 miles (1,390 m) long, the second longest in Europe. It originates in the Swiss Alps and flows northward to the North Sea. The river forms a natural border between Germany and Switzerland from Lake Constance to the Swiss town of Basel, it continues between France and Germany from Basel to Karlsruhe. Breathtaking vineyards, fortresses, castles, and picturesque towns line the banks of the Rhine.

The river is navigable for about 540 miles (870 km). It is the busiest waterway in Europe—ships traveling on the Rhine carry 183.6 million tons of cargo every year. In the Alps, the river moves rapidly, turning into spectacular waterfalls at Schaffhausen, Switzerland. It then opens onto a wide plateau from Karlsruhe to Mainz, where crops are grown along its banks. North of Mainz, the river plunges into a gorge through the Schiefergebirge before opening out into a wider flood plain to the north of Koblenz, the traditional wine-growing region. Between Cologne and the Dutch border, the Rhine flows through the Ruhr industrial area.

EAST AND WEST

The division of Germany into East—the Deutsche Demokratische Republik (DOY-cher demm-oh-CRATT-ish-e rep-oo-BLEEK)—and West—the Bundesrepublik Deutschland (BOON-dess Rep-oo-BLEEK DOY-chs-lant)—between 1945 and 1990 affected every part of German life and geography. Even today, it is still in a phase of rapid change.

Agricultural development, landholding patterns, industrial practice, housing, and forms of law enforcement and government all differed greatly from East to West.

Environmental concerns about industrial pollution, long overdue efforts to preserve historical buildings, maintaining housing in adequate condition, and restoring land seized by the former East German state from families are just some of the issues Germany has been trying to resolve. Together with the very visible contrasts between the two former states, social and economic problems are arising from different attitudes toward work, wealth, goals, and standard of living.

The Neuschwanstein Castle in Bavaria was the inspiration for Disneyland's castle. The romantic site is a popular stop for tourist cruises sailing on the Rhine.

THE BERLIN WALL

East Germany was the part of Germany that came under Soviet rule at the end of World War II. This area had suffered some of the worst wartime bomb damage and was also forced to make extremely demanding compensation payments to the Allied nations for Germany's actions in the war. It experienced an almost immediate population drain to West Germany after World War II.

During the early 1950s, the border between the two states was guarded by watch towers and barbed wire from the Eastern side, but a steady stream of emigrants, totalling about 3.5 million, continued to leave through Berlin. On August 13, 1961, an 11-foot (3.3-m) high concrete wall was constructed overnight, dividing the Communist East from the West. The wall became a symbol of the oppression of the East German regime, turning the former capital into a divided city as the main street—Unter den Linden—was blocked by part of the 40-mile (64-km) barrier. At least 72 people died attempting to cross the wall, 55 of whom were shot by East German security forces. The last victim, Chris Gueffroy, was shot in February 1989.

In the late 1980s, popular protests began, ending with the fall of the communist government and the opening of the wall on November 9, 1989. When the wall opened, a flood of Germans from both East and West streamed through. Parts of the wall still stand in some places in Berlin, and a section of it is on display at the Memorial of the Division on Bernauer Strasse (*above*).

STATES

Before reunification, West Germany was divided into 10 states. These states remain in today's united country. From north to south, they are Schleswig-Holstein, with Kiel as its capital; Lower Saxony, with Hannover; North Rhine-Westphalia, with Düsseldorf; Hesse, with Wiesbaden; Rhineland-Palatinate, with Mainz; Saarland, with Saarbrücken; Baden-Württemberg, with Stuttgart; Bavaria, with Munich; and the city states of Hamburg and Bremen. West Berlin was the 11th state, but had a different legal status, technically administered and defended by the World War II victors France, Britain, and the United States.

The former East German states of Mecklenburg-Western Pomerania, Brandenburg, Saxony, Thuringia, and Saxony-Anhalt were turned into 14 administrative districts by the Communist regime. Since reunification, these districts have gone back to their original statehoods, and East and West Berlin have been joined into a single new city-state, which is also the capital of Germany.

Vineyards cover the hills of a wine-making town in the state of Hesse

A modern sculpture at the City Center in Berlin. In the distance stands the Memorial Church, which was badly damaged during World War II.

CITIES

There is no single dominant city in Germany, which has a strong tradition of local self-government. Wealth, industry, and cultural activities are spread around the whole country, preventing the common problem of overconcentration of resources in one area at the expense of others.

BERLIN The formerly divided city is once again an artistic and cultural center, with over 200 musical groups, an annual jazz festival, alternative modern artists and fringe theaters, left-wing thinkers, and radical supporters of the peace movement. Berlin has a large gay community. It also has the largest Turkish population of any city outside Turkey.

The Kurfürstendamm is a two-mile (3.2-km) long street in the amusement and shopping district of the city, where shops stay open late. In 1991, Germany voted to return its capital from Bonn to Berlin. The German national parliament, the *Bundestag* (BOON-des-tahg), moved back to its original home in Berlin, the newly-restored Reichstag, in 1999.

MUNICH A cultural and intellectual city, it is also an international fashion capital and a world-renowned brewing center. The city center is only one mile (1.6 km) across, and no skyscrapers are allowed to interrupt the original style of architecture. Munich hosted the 1972 Olympics. Its sports and leisure facilities are excellent, as is its transportation system. Siemens, one of the world's leading electrical engineering and electronics companies, BMW, and MBB Aerospace are based in Munich.

STUTTGART Set in a picturesque hollow of terraced suburbs surrounded by vineyards and forested hills, Stuttgart feels small despite a surrounding industrial area that houses major companies like Bosch, DaimlerChrysler, Porsche, and German IBM. The downtown area is relatively new, as it was rebuilt after World War II. Stuttgart has a famous ballet troupe, several foreign consulates, and inviting open-air cafés along the Schlossplatz, the central pedestrian zone.

FRANKFURT-AM-MAIN The city has been a banking center since the 16th century. The German Stock Exchange, the headquarters of most German banks, and the European Central Bank are located in Frankfurt's city center. The city's trade revenue supports a generous budget for the arts, architecture, and conservation. It is also a publishing center and the host of the biggest annual international book fair every October. Frankfurt is an international city with a bright intellectual life. Twenty-two percent of its population are immigrant workers. The city also operates the largest airport in Germany and one of the busiest in Europe.

Lovely red flowers line a park in Stuttgart.

The sharp towers of Cologne's cathedral define the city's skyline.

BONN This old university town was the capital of former West Germany from 1945 to 1991. Many of its residents are university professors, students, and retired government civil servants. Beethoven's birthplace, the Beethovenhaus, has been turned into a museum; it houses the instruments, scores, and memorabilia of the famous composer. Since the move of the capital to Berlin in 1999, Bonn has experienced an economic downturn.

COLOGNE Once the ancient Roman empire's leading colony, several Romanesque churches as well as a world-famous cathedral have survived. The city was badly damaged during World War II—90 percent of the city center was destroyed—and poorly planned postwar architecture has kept it from regaining its former beauty. Nevertheless, Cologne is an open and friendly city with several museums, a lively art market, and a spectacular carnival. Cologne also hosts the biggest pop-music fair in Europe called Popkomm. Held every summer for a week, the festival attracts musicians, pop stars, and record companies from Europe.

A tourist boat on the Elbe River sails past the city of Dresden.

HAMBURG Germany's second largest city is built on water and has 2,195 bridges that cross over the Elbe River, Lake Alster, and many canals. The lake freezes over during the winter. There are few high-rise buildings in the city center, which makes use of mostly red-brick architecture, and the tallest buildings are approximately 30 stories high. The once prosperous port is struggling to compete with Rotterdam, in the Netherlands, and is hampered by the European Union tariff regulations.

DRESDEN The site of the worst bombing during the last stages of World War II, Dresden was almost completely destroyed. Although some of its older buildings were rebuilt, present-day Dresden displays an unattractive mixture of postwar structures—many of which need replacing—and a few older buildings. Under the Communist regime, the buildings that survived Allied bombs fell into disrepair, and several, including the Stadtschloss (dating from 1443), were destroyed. Following reunification, unemployment and unrest have resulted in growing extremist activity in the city.

The town of Heidelberg in the Rhine rift valley is covered in snow during winter.

CLIMATE

The northwest region of Germany has an Atlantic climate similar to that of the American Northwest: westerly winds, cool summers, moderate winters, high humidity, and a high annual rainfall.

In the northeast, the winters are bitterly cold, as the area receives the force of the Russian winds, with hot summers and relatively low rainfall.

The Alpine region is characterized by warm but short summers and cold, snowy winters. Mild, warm winds, known as the foehns, blowing in from the south are responsible for the melting of snow at the end of winter.

The climate in the Rhine rift valley, which has an early spring, light rainfall, warm summers, and few frosts, is ideal for agriculture as well as tourism. Average January temperatures are 35°F (1.6°C) in the lowlands and 21°F (-6°C) in the mountains. In the summer, the temperatures are 63°F (17°C) in the mountains and 68°F (20°C) in the upper Rhine valley. The driest month is February. The average annual rainfall in the Central German Uplands is 58 inches (1.5 m).

FLORA AND FAUNA

Forests cover 30 percent of Germany, and all are open to the public. About 45 percent of the forests are pine, 40 percent beech, and 8 percent oak. Forests that receive enough light and have good soil offer favorable conditions for the growth of dog's mercury, sweet woodruff, and violets. At higher levels, balsam, willow herb, monkshood, bilberry, foxgloves, and wavy hair grass are found.

Flowers in full bloom in the German countryside

In 1980, the first signs of pollution became evident when trees were found to be dying. Acid rain caused by sulfur dioxide emissions from industry was believed to be the cause. These dying forests are one of Germany's most important ecological issues. Regulations to reduce pollution caused by cars have been introduced to try to prevent further damage.

The government has strict antipollution laws; industries face heavy fines for discharging poisonous emissions. The Rhine River and its valley underwent a successful cleanup campaign: the waters of the river were made clean enough for the pollution-sensitive salmon to grow and thrive. In addition, various nature conservation groups advised using natural rather than chemical pesticides to rid the area of insects.

Some of the former border territories between East and West Germany have been turned into nature reserves. A 5,680-acre (2,300-hectare) area along Lake Schaal between Schleswig-Holstein and Mecklenburg hosts sea eagles, cranes, cormorants, bitterns, greylag geese, osprey, and other birds. Much of the Lüneburg heath region in the northeast is a nature reserve, as is the Bavarian National Park. Wild boar and deer are hunted in Bavaria, and deer are also found in mountainous areas, such as the Harz Mountains and the Alpine Foothills.

HISTORY

THE HISTORY OF GERMANY AS A NATION is relatively short, since the country was first united as a nation in 1871. The history of the German people, however, dates back to ancient times.

EARLY HISTORY

During the Bronze Age, Germanic peoples probably inhabited southern Scandinavia and northern Germany. Around the first century A.D., the Roman Empire attempted to expand its territory in the northeast, but were driven away by the German Cherusci tribe leader Arminius in A.D. 9. The Romans tried to keep the Germanic tribes at bay by using the Rhine and Danube rivers as natural barriers, further reinforcing these with a 341-mile-long (550-km-long) wall called the Limes. Parts of this wall can still be seen today.

The arrival of the Huns at the end of the third century forced the migration of Germanic tribes— Ostrogoths, Visigoths, and Vandals—into Roman territory, in what became known as the *Völkerwanderung* (FOLL-ker-van-der-ung). The Vandals crossed the Rhine River in A.D. 46, bringing an end to Roman rule in the region. The Vandals, Goths, and other Germanic tribes settled there in the second half of the fourth century.

At the end of the fifth century, the neighboring Franks under the Merovingian king, Clovis I, expanded political control over territories from northern Spain and the Atlantic coast to the Rhine, converting all the people to Christianity. By the beginning of the eighth century, the Franks had conquered all the Germanic tribes except the Saxons.

Above: **A medieval castle stands overlooking the Rhine River.**

Opposite: **The old Rathaus (city hall) in Bamberg, Bavaria, was built on an islet on the Regnitz River.**

THE MIDDLE AGES

Charlemagne, known in Germany as Karl der Grosse (ruled 768–814), was crowned Holy Roman Emperor by the pope in A.D. 800. He conquered and converted the Saxons to Christianity in 805. After Charlemagne's death, the kingdom of the Eastern Franks became the Germanic kingdom under Ludwig the German (843–876); the area of the Western Franks became what is now France; and the land in the middle, Lotharingia, became Lorraine.

Later, another German king, Otto I the Great (936–973), defeated the Hungarian Magyars at Lechfeld in 955, conquered northern Italy, and was crowned Holy Roman Emperor in 962. From then until 1806, all German kings were given this title. The church became an administrative part of the empire, gaining wealth, land, and importance.

Under Heinrich IV (1056–1106), a dispute arose with the pope, leading to a split of the Christian empire and disunity among the German princes within the Germanic kingdom. Friedrich I of the Hohenstaufen dynasty, also known as Barbarossa (1152–1190), started wars against the pope, the Italians, and the Saxons, but the rise of individual German princes and dukes weakened the dynasty and led to the end of the Hohenstaufen era in 1268; the kings eventually became a pawn of the powerful aristocrats. Throughout the 12th and 13th centuries, Germanic influence increased east of the Elbe River, and Teutonic knights spread Christianity along most of the Baltic coasts. In 1356, the empire established rules for electing the king of Germany. Princes and dukes had votes, as did the archbishop of Mainz and some important towns.

Hohenschwangen castle in Bavaria is a medieval fortress which was rebuilt in the 19th century.

THE HAPSBURG DYNASTY

With the rise of the Hapsburg dynasty in Austria, political power in Germany shifted to eastern Germany, but the Rhineland princes and dukes continued to exert political influence. The Hapsburg dynasty also increased the emperor's powers. Rudolf I (ruled 1273–91) virtually controlled Germany and Austria. The next Hapsburg rulers, Maximilian I (1493–1519) and his grandson Charles V (1519–56), were both powerful Holy Roman emperors.

In 1517, during the Hapsburg's reign, Martin Luther, a friar, wrote the Ninety-Five Theses to protest the various abuses in the Catholic Church, in particular the sale of "indulgences" for the forgiveness of sins. Luther's strong criticism of the Church sparked the Protestant Reformation.

Many princes and dukes became Protestant, and religious wars were fought until the Peace of Augsburg, which allowed Protestants the same rights of worship as Catholics, was signed in 1555. Although four-fifths of Germany had become Protestant, the ratio changed after many of the abuses were corrected during the Counter Reformation started by the Council of Trent (1545–63).

Peace did not last for long. The Thirty Years' War (1618–48), fueled by religious hatred within Germany, ended in the Treaty of Westphalia. But the war reduced the population by one-third. The treaty took away much of the remaining power of the Hapsburg kings. It also deprived Germany of access to the sea, leaving 1,800 independent kingdoms. Some of the rulers of these kingdoms, including Frederick the Great II of Prussia (1640–88) and Joseph II of Austria (1765–90), encouraged humanistic inquiry.

The church door at Wittenberg, where Martin Luther allegedly posted his Ninety-Five Theses.

NINETEENTH-CENTURY GERMANY

The French Revolution of 1789 had its effect in Germany. When the left bank of the Rhine River and Berlin were occupied during the Napoleonic Wars and the last Holy Roman emperor, Franz II, was forced from the throne in 1806, the fires of German nationalism were lit.

The Congress of Vienna convened in 1815 at the end of the Napoleonic Wars. For nine months, the Congress strove to redraw the political boundaries of Europe. A German Confederation of 39 states, which included Austria, was formed. In 1834 the German Customs Union was formed. Austria opted to stay out, but smaller states joined, creating a single inland market that replaced a whole range of customs, currencies, and controls.

The state of Brandenburg-Prussia expanded its power during the second half of the 19th century under the leadership of its prime minister, Otto von Bismarck. The brief German-Danish War of 1864 gained Schleswig and Holstein for Prussia and Austria. In 1866, Prussia defeated Austria to secure these lands after a dispute over their control, emerging as the most powerful state in Germany.

Prussia subsequently dissolved the German Confederation and replaced it with the North German Federation. Bismarck was chosen chancellor of this federation, and in 1870, a short, victorious war with France added the provinces of Alsace and Lorraine. The southern German states later joined their northern neighbors, forming the German empire, or *Reich* (RIKE). On January 18, 1871, King William I of Prussia became the *Kaiser* (KYE-zer), or German emperor, of an empire of 25 states.

Otto von Bismarck (1815–98) was an able Prussian diplomat who later served as prime minister of Prussia. He masterminded the creation of a united German state and became the first German chancellor.

WORLD WAR I

Longing to have overseas colonies like that of Britain and France, Germany rebuilt its navy. As Germany's military was already the most powerful in Europe, the country's colonial ambitions troubled its neighbors. In 1907, Britain, France, and Russia formed an alliance called the Triple Entente.

War was sparked off by the assassination of Archduke Franz Ferdinand, the heir to the Austrian throne, in Serbia in June 1914. Austria invaded Serbia with German support, while Russia, supported by France, sided with Serbia. Germany declared war on France, invading Belgium in order to destroy French defenses. Britain entered the war in defense of Belgium.

World War I turned out to be the worst war Europe had ever seen. Fighting in the trenches in northeastern France lasted for four years, with terrible casualties on both sides. The United States' entry into the war in 1917 helped turn the tide against Germany and its allies.

Following a ceasefire, a treaty was signed and World War I ended in November 1918. Kaiser William II gave up his throne and fled.

German artillery firing at French troops during the height of the Battle of Verdun in 1916. This battle, which cost the lives of hundreds of thousands of German and French soldiers, was one of the most terrible in history.

RESULTS OF WORLD WAR I The Treaty of Versailles held Germany and its allies fully responsible for the war. The victors imposed reparations (war payments) and tried to prevent a future rise of the German military.

In the war and subsequent peace, Germany lost 27,000 square miles (70,000 square km) of territory, 7.2 million people, 15 percent of its farming output, 10 percent of its manufacturing capacity, 75 percent of its iron ore production, and all its overseas colonies. East and West Prussia were separated to allow Poland access to the Baltic Sea, and Danzig (now Gdansk in Poland) was declared a free city. Alsace-Lorraine went to France, which also occupied the coal-rich Saarland area. Three million ethnic Germans were left outside German territory.

From left to right: **Field Marshall Paul von Hindenburg, Kaiser William II, and General Erich Ludendorff in the German headquarters planning an assault against the Allies during World War I. Hindenburg later became the president of Germany.**

Unemployed Germans collect food stamps in 1932.

THE WEIMAR REPUBLIC

Following its devastating military defeat, a provisional government tasked with drafting a democratic constitution for the new German republic was set up in the city of Weimar. Well-meaning but ultimately unconvincing Social Democrat politicians attempted to put the country back on its feet, but the loss of Alsace-Lorraine to France and the heavy reparations burden crippled the country economically. In 1923, Germany could not pay its reparations, which led France to occupy the Ruhr coalfields to extract its own form of compensation.

Morale dropped drastically, and inflation reached astronomic proportions, virtually leading the country into a barter economy where goods were exchanged. The US Stock Market crash of 1929 and the Great Depression that followed affected the German economy, leaving Germany with 7 million unemployed. These harsh socio-economic conditions led to the rise of extremist groups.

THE HITLER YEARS

The National Socialist Party movement, or the Nazis, an extreme right-wing organization led by Adolf Hitler, opposed Communism and blamed Jewish bankers and financiers, as well as France's hostile reparations demands, for Germany's plight. Support for the Nazis grew, and by 1932 they had become the strongest party in parliament.

On January 30, 1933, Hitler was appointed chancellor by President Hindenburg. In 1934, Hindenburg died and Hitler proclaimed himself leader, or *Führer* (FYUR-er), with almost absolute powers. In 1935, the Saarland voted to return to Germany, and the following year Hitler defied the Versailles peace terms by remilitarizing the Rhine area. This policy had gained popularity for the Nazi party among the people, as desperately needed jobs were created in arms manufacturing and highway construction.

Dachau concentration camp near Munich has been turned into a memorial site, where visitors can enter and take a tour of the facility free of charge. A poignant sign on one of the walls of the camp reads "Never Again" in five languages, Hebrew, French, English, German, and Russian.

Hitler's insane vision of German racial supremacy began to take shape. He sought to "purify" the Aryan race by selective genetic breeding and the destruction of the Jews. German Jews were arrested and their businesses destroyed. During the early 1940s, the Nazis sent millions of Jews to concentration camps where most were tortured and killed.

WORLD WAR II Hitler's aim of creating a mighty German state began in 1938 with the annexation of Austria, followed by parts of Czechoslovakia. On September 1, 1939, World War II began when Germany invaded Poland. Britain and France, Poland's allies, immediately declared war on Germany. Poland was defeated and former Prussian lands were "returned" to Germany. Hitler's armies conquered Denmark and Norway, followed by Belgium, the Netherlands, France, Yugoslavia, and Greece. In 1940, Germany and Italy formed an alliance. In 1941, Hitler turned against his former ally, the Soviet Union, and invaded Russia. When Japan attacked Pearl Harbor in December 1941, Germany declared war on the United States.

The city of Dresden was left in rubble after the terrible firebombing by Allied planes in 1945.

In late 1942, the German armies suffered terrible losses in the Soviet Union and North Africa. In 1943, Allied troops from the United States and Britain, who had formed a military alliance, defeated Italy. Allied troops landed in France in 1944 and swept into Germany. From the east, Soviet armies drove to Berlin. On April 30, 1945, surrounded on all sides, Hitler committed suicide and Germany surrendered.

POSTWAR GERMANY

Immediately after its surrender, Germany was demilitarized and divided into four administrative zones by France, Britain, the United States, and the Soviet Union. An agreement on how to govern Germany was reached in late 1945. Britain, France, and the United States would govern the western two-thirds of Germany, and the Soviet Union would govern the eastern one third. Within the Russian zone lay the historic capital, Berlin, which was also divided into four administrative zones. All of northeastern Prussia went to the Soviet Union and all German territories east of the Oder River were under Polish control. As a result about 9.5 million Germans living in the eastern regions were expelled and forced to immigrate to West Germany. As many as 1 million people may have died on the way.

With the start of the Cold War between the East and the West, the Allies' concerns shifted from German reconstruction to stopping the spread of communism. In 1948, the western zones were turned into the Federal Republic of Germany; the following year Konrad Adenauer was appointed its first federal chancellor. This country was regarded as a temporary solution until the eastern section joined it. In time the Soviet-occupied zone became the Democratic Republic of Germany.

West Germany remained occupied and only attained self-rule in 1955. East Germans came under the rule of the Socialist Unity Party (SED), or the East German Communist Party, led by Walter Ulbricht.

EAST-WEST GERMAN RELATIONS

With the introduction of communist principles, the redistribution of land and wealth, and the Soviet Union's crippling reparations demands, thousands of East Germans were forced to cross to the wealthier West. Aside from economic reasons, many families were divided by the new

West Germany was rapidly restored by the Allies after World War II. It joined the North Atlantic Treaty Organization (NATO) in the 1950s, reforming its army in 1956. In 1963, United States president John F. Kennedy visited the country to develop close relations, and summed up his feelings during a visit to Berlin: "Ich bin ein Berliner!" ("I am a Berliner.")

border. In June 1953, a revolt in East Berlin and other East German towns was put down by Soviet troops. The 855-mile (1,375-km) border between East and West Germany was fortified to become a guarded barrier, which became known as the Iron Curtain. In 1961, the Berlin Wall was built.

During the 1960s, at the height of the Cold War, there was little communication between the two Germanys. Later that decade, Chancellor Willy Brandt of West Germany started *Ostpolitik* (OST-poll-ee-teek), a program of meeting with the East German government to improve relations between East and West Germany. A few years later, a treaty was signed. West German citizens were allowed to visit relatives in the East for limited periods, but East Germans were not allowed to travel to the West.

THE BERLIN AIRLIFT

When West Germany introduced radical postwar currency reform in 1948, Soviet leader Josef Stalin attempted to win the whole city for the Communist East by imposing a blockade.

In June 1948, the Soviet Union blockaded the western part of Berlin, closing all land corridors and railway access to the city from the west. As food, fuel, and raw materials needed in the factories were transported from the western side of the country, the blockade left Berliners without access to basic supplies.

The blockade lasted 10 months, from June 1948 to May 1949. The gamble failed because the Western Allied powers began an around-the-clock airlift into the city. Western planes flew a total of 120,000 flights into West Berlin, bringing 1.5 million tons of food, medical supplies, and other essentials to supply the 2 million inhabitants. Eventually, Soviet leader Josef Stalin realized that he would not succeed in overtaking the city in this manner, so he ordered the blockade to be lifted.

REUNIFICATION

The West German constitution had always regarded the division of Germany as temporary and provided for the reunification of the country. West Germany always welcomed all East German refugees who did manage the incredibly difficult passage across the border as citizens.

When Mikhail Gorbachev started his policy of glasnost, translated as openness, in the Soviet Union in the late 1980s, the gradual decrease of Soviet control over East Germany and Eastern Europe led to peaceful revolutions.

In May 1989, East Germans on vacation in Hungary took advantage of the country's newly opened borders and crossed via Austria into West Germany. Other East Germans sought refuge at West German embassies in Czechoslovakia and Poland. Later that year, the first steps toward reunification were taken when East German travel restrictions were lifted. A visit by Gorbachev in October 1989 made it clear that Soviet troops would no longer support the country. Barely a month later, the Berlin Wall was torn down. Talks on reunification between the East and West German governments progressed rapidly, and a treaty of unification was signed on October 3, 1990.

The first full democratic parliamentary elections took place two months later, in which East and West Germans voted together as one country, electing Helmut Kohl as chancellor of a reunified Germany. Uniting Germany economically and socially has been more complicated and has demanded more time than many had expected during the euphoria from 1989 to 1990. Forty years of separation resulted in the development of different political, economic, and social institutions. Even as the eastern and western halves of the country come to share increasingly more in common, German reunification remains a work in progress

East meets West. Former East German leader Erich Honecker (*left*) meets Helmut Kohl (*right*), the first chancellor of united Germany.

GOVERNMENT

GERMANY HAS A FEDERAL, decentralized system of government, in which each state, or *Land* (LAHND), has the right to govern its citizens independently from the central government. Each state has its own constitution, although its regulations must fall within the guidelines laid down in the Basic Law, Germany's set of governing laws that were established in 1949.

FEDERAL GOVERNMENT

The federal style of government has its roots in the theories of 15th century Dutch Calvinist political thinker Johannes Althusius. He advocated the right of every social group to provide for the well-being of its members. In its modern-day form, a federal government allows a wide application of democratic principles on the local and national level.

Above: **Germany's chancellor, Helmut Schroeder, leader of the Social Democratic Party.**

Opposite: **Two policemen patrol the streets of Cologne on horseback, a common mode of police patrol in the city.**

The federal system allows for many checks and balances on the central power. For example, the head of the German government—the federal chancellor—is in charge of the armed forces only in times of war; during peacetime, the army is under the control of the federal minister of defense.

There are two houses of government in Germany: the *Bundestag*, which consists of 603 members elected by citizens every four years, which in turn elects the federal chancellor; and the *Bundesrat* (BOON-des-raht), made up of nominees from the state governments that represent the interests of the states. Voting is not compulsory, but anyone above age 18 has the right to vote. The German president is the head of state, elected every five years by the federal assembly and the state representatives. The president officially appoints the federal chancellor once the latter is elected by the *Bundestag*.

The newly rebuilt German Reichstag in Berlin boasts an impressive crystal dome, which is meant to represent the transparency of German politics.

In June 1991, the German parliament voted to move the *Bundestag* from its premises in Bonn to Berlin. In September 1999 the parliament held its inaugural session in the Reichstag in Berlin. The *Bundesrat* has also moved to a newly renovated historical building in Berlin. The federal government is responsible for defense, foreign policy, transportation, postal services, currency, trade tariffs, and issuing passports. It shares duties with the state governments for civil and criminal law enforcement, labor law, road traffic, and economic matters, having the right to legislate when necessary, to ensure uniform laws for the whole country. Income from taxes is divided between the federal and state governments.

Former West Germany joined the North Atlantic Treaty Organization (NATO) in 1954 and the United Nations in 1973. Its army, the *Bundeswehr* (BOON-des-vare), is a purely defensive force, meaning it is not allowed to start an attack unless directly provoked. All German men must give 12 months of national service. Conscientious objectors (those who do not want to serve in the army for moral principles) can do social work instead.

STATE GOVERNMENTS

Each of the states has its own elected parliament—called *Landesrat* (LAHND-es-raht). As with the federal government, voting is optional, and all citizens over 18 have the right to vote.

The state governments are responsible for health care, education policies, broadcasting, and cultural affairs. They make and administer local laws and environmental protection measures, run their own police forces, and enforce traffic regulations and federal laws.

The local governments in turn look after the towns, communities, and counties. Mayors are well paid so as to attract talented individuals to such positions.

The local authorities collect certain taxes and share in others, although each state grants them additional revenues to keep solvent. Revenue problems frequently arise at the state level. For instance, the city state of Hamburg has high property taxes; people who purposely live just outside its borders and commute pay lower rates to the state, which decreases Hamburg's revenue.

The eastern states (former East Germany) still depend heavily on funds from the federal government in order to sustain a standard of living comparable to that enjoyed by the western states. Large sums of money are needed to improve and restore housing, upgrade industries, and make local economies competitive.

The public and private sector have put together a massive program of aid and investment to assist the former East Germany. Transfers to the new eastern states from the West total $70 billion every year.

The headquarters of Jena, one of the most successful companies in the former East Germany.

A SDP political rally in Cologne.

POLITICAL PARTIES

There are five major political parties in Germany. The Christian Democratic Union (CDU) and the Christian Social Union (CSU) from Bavaria form one parliamentary block, drawing support from Protestants and Catholics. The CDU, former chancellor Kohl's party, initially gained large-scale support in East Germany. The Social Democratic Party (SPD) has been in power since 1998, with Chancellor Gerhard Schroeder as its head. The Free Democratic Party (FDP) and the Green Party make up the rest. The German Communist Party (KPD), which was banned in 1923 but resurfaced as the Socialist Unity Party (SED), was the party in power in former East Germany from 1945 to 1990.

There are various smaller political parties, generally more powerful at the state than at the federal level. But their political power is hampered by a law that states that only parties that have gained 5 percent or more of the votes in an election can send representatives to the *Bundestag*—a check that has so far stopped extreme right- and left-wing parties from gaining seats.

THE LEGAL SYSTEM

Germany has a highly regulated society. Citizens must carry identification cards or papers, drive with their license and insurance documents, and can be fined for crossing the road where there is no pedestrian crossing.

The Basic Law lays out numerous rules to protect democracy and freedom of speech and guarantees a catalog of human rights that includes the protection of political refugees. There is no death penalty in Germany.

There are six different types of courts: the ordinary court for criminal and civil cases; the labor court for labor relations; the administrative court for all administrative laws; the social court for social programs; the fiscal court for tax matters; and the federal constitutional court, which is the highest court of appeal as well as a constitutional and legislative body.

REUNIFICATION The legal system in former East Germany was one of the many complex issues that needed to be solved during reunification. All judges and lawyers in East Germany were trained in the highly political communist system. There was evidence that many of these officials were guilty of maltreatment and torture of prisoners. As many of the judges had to be dismissed, former judges in the West had to be brought out of retirement in order to fill up the vacancies in the East.

The ordinary police force was unwilling to do more than keep order until their role in the new Germany was confirmed. The former East German secret police, the *Stasi* (STAH-zee), kept numerous files on German citizens. Its former members, along with roughly 5,000 former East German spies, were brought to trial for past crimes.

THE GREENS

In 1983, the Green Party, which evolved from a radical environmental protection movement, won its first seats in the *Bundestag*. It has won seats in all federal and many state parliaments since. The party campaigns on nuclear issues, industrial pollution, saving the natural heritage, and pacifism. Its social and welfare programs include the belief that each individual should receive an income, whether or not he or she has a job. The party has inspired other groups in Europe and has succeeded in bringing environmental issues into the political scene.

ECONOMY

GERMANY IS THE WORLD'S third largest economy, after the United States and Japan. As such, Germany is the leading economic and technological power in the European Union.

Due to worldwide recession and the cost of reabsorbing the people and inefficient industries of former East Germany, the impressive economic growth rate posted by Germany since the 1950s experienced a temporary decline in the 1990s. Since reunification, the growth rate has been consistently low. In 2002, the growth rate fell to under 1 percent.

In January 2002, Germany, along with 11 other EU member countries, replaced its official currency, the deutsch mark, with the euro.

Left: **Downtown Frankfurt, the financial center of Germany.**

Opposite: **The BMW Tower in Munich.**

Farmers plant potatoes in Mecklenburg.

POSTWAR ECONOMIC MIRACLE

Over half of West Germany's industrial capacity was destroyed during World War II, and a further 5 percent was taken from existing capital and foreign assets as part of war payments. In East Germany, the Soviet Union moved currency production, and sometimes entire plants, to the USSR.

During the 1950s, West Germany experienced fantastic economic growth. The *Wirtschaftswunder* (VIRT-shafts-voon-der), or economic miracle, was largely the result of the hard work and determination of the German people to succeed. The country reached economic stability by 1953, and full employment by 1959. And industrial production rose by 130 percent in the late 1950s.

Other factors contributed to this success. The Marshall Plan, started by the United States, provided economic aid. A bold currency reform attacked inflation. Price and wage controls were abolished, and a sensible industrial relations policy was achieved. The Korean War in the 1950s increased demand for manufactured goods.

INFRASTRUCTURE AND COMMUNICATIONS

Present-day Germany has a highly effective infrastructure and communications system. The federal government owns and subsidizes the postal services. The railways were also state-owned until 1994, when they were privatized. At that time, a total of 27,300 miles (44,000 km) of railway tracks ran across the country

A positive outcome of the Nazi era is the solid infrastructure of roads and highways, known as *Autobahn* (AW-toh-bahn). This network spreads out from Berlin throughout all of Germany. It expanded rapidly during former West Germany's car boom period of the 1950s, and remains a spectacular achievement, with a network of about 7,000 miles (11,400 km) of highways. There is currently no speed limit for cars on some of the highways, although certain restrictions do apply.

Germany also has an extensive network of inland waterways—rivers and canals—linking the industrial towns of the Rhine River with the Baltic ports and the rest of the European market. For instance, 25 percent of manufactured and agricultural goods are transported on water, of which 70 percent goes through the Rhine River. The Nord-Ostsee Canal across the state of Schleswig-Holstein is a busy route for goods traveling between the Baltic and North Seas.

Lufthansa, the national airline, was privatized in 1997 when the government sold its 37.5 share in the company. As for telecommunications and satellites, Germany has some of the most efficient in the world.

A barge enters a lock in the canal at Magdeburg.

THE GERMAN CAR INDUSTRY

The German car industry is the largest in Europe. In 2002, 5.1 million vehicles were produced, of which about two-thirds were sold to other countries. Only Japan produces more cars each year.

The greatest success of the German car industry has been in the area of expensive high performance vehicles. Probably the most famous luxury car in the world today, the Mercedes-Benz, had its beginnings in Germany. A man named Gottlieb Daimler invented the gasoline engine in the 1880s in the city of Stuttgart, while another, Karl Benz, was starting similar developments some 80 miles (128 km) away in Mannheim.

Emil Jellinek, a diplomat and a major investor in Daimler's firm, suggested that Daimler's new line of luxury cars, which sported a four-cylinder engine, be named after Jellinek's daughter Mercedes. Jellinek feared that the German-sounding Daimler name would not appeal to the French. In 1901, Daimler sold the first Mercedes car. Although the Daimler and Benz companies (*above*) only fully merged in 1960, Mercedes-Benz has been a household name around the world for decades. In 1998, the biggest merger of two industrial companies in history took place when Daimler-Benz joined American car manufacturer Chrysler to form DaimlerChrysler.

Another famous German car company, Bayerische Motoren Werke, more commonly known as BMW, made aircraft engines during World War I, then expanded into motorcycles and sports cars. But in the 1950s, its future was uncertain until the main shareholders—the Quandt family—took over and made it the automobile power that it is today.

The product of another German car company rivals that of Daimler-Benz as the most famous German car in the world. In 1938, Volkswagen (meaning people's car) started mass production of an automobile designed in 1936 by an Austrian named Ferdinand Porsche—the "beetle." The company remained fully nationalized until 1961, but its sales started to slip as Germans became wealthier and could afford luxury cars. To meet this challenge, Volkswagen developed the "yuppie car" of the 1980s, the best-selling Volkswagen Golf.

Volkswagen has ties with two other famous cars. First, the company owns Audi, producers of a popular luxury car. Second, when Ferdinand Porsche left Volkswagen in the 1950s, he started his own car company. Sports car lovers admire the sleek design of Porsche. In 2001, 50 percent of Porsche's total sales was to the United States. The company is still run by the Porsche family.

In contrast with West Germany's successful car industry, the former East German car company Trabant closed down shortly after German reunification, when faced with strong competition from the other more established and famous car makers. As a result, 1 million jobs were lost.

The DaimlerChrysler factory is located near Stuttgart.

INDUSTRIES

As it lacks significant natural resources, Germany must import most of its raw materials and energy sources. It does, however, have profitable bituminous and brown coal (lignite) deposits in the Ruhr and Saar valleys. Germany's steel industry is concentrated near these areas. The country also has small amounts of iron ore, petroleum, and natural gas.

The chemical industry is one of Germany's major industries. It includes world-famous companies like Bayer and BASF. Machine and vehicle construction is another major industrial sector and includes aircraft manufacture, shipbuilding, plant machinery, and, of course, automobiles.

Electrical engineering, electronics, and office equipment are growing industrial sectors. Although many industries are extremely successful, traditional heavy industries such as steel and shipbuilding are, as in other Western countries, suffering a severe decline. Competition from the Japanese and new technology are reducing the profits enjoyed by German production. In 2002, industrial output accounted for 31 percent of the value of Germany's total gross domestic product (GDP).

AGRICULTURE

As with other Western countries, a decreasing proportion of Germany's population works on the land. Farms are growing larger and are often linked together in cooperatives, although many small-scale operations remain, often run by part-timers with other jobs.

The different regions and soil types are suited to different types of farming. The north coast, with marshy soil rich in nutrients, is suited for dairy farming and some horse breeding. Pasture lands are found on the foothills of the Alps. Poultry, pigs, cattle, and some sheep and ducks are raised in these areas. A fertile belt runs along the southern flank of the lowlands, with crops such as wheat and feed grains for livestock, vegetables, sugar beet, fruits, potatoes, and grapes that produce wine. Bavaria, Hesse, Baden-Württemberg, and Rhineland-Palatinate have forestry farming.

Farming in Germany is regulated by the Common Agricultural Policy of the European Union, which at first encouraged overproduction of grain crops but is now penalizing overproduction to maintain falling farm prices. Fishing in the North Sea is also governed by numerous regulations.

Vineyards above the town of Rüdesheim offer beautiful scenery.

The Deutsche Bank building in Frankfurt.

TRADE AND COMMERCE

Wholesale trade continues to flourish in Germany, although many small enterprises have gone out of business because they were unable to offer the services and discounts of larger operators. Retail turnover has been growing, and self-service operations are replacing more traditional trade outlets.

Foreign trade has been a major factor in Germany's economic success, with a liberal policy aimed at breaking down trade barriers. Machinery, motor vehicles, chemical products, precision and optical goods, and electrical engineering goods are its main exports. Food, drinks, textiles, and petroleum products are its main imports.

The bulk of Germany's trade is within the European Union. Major trade fairs are held in Hannover, mainly for mechanical and industrial products.

Although the cost of reunification has slowed economic growth in the country, Germany posted a trade surplus of 9 billion euros for the year 2002.

BANKING AND FINANCE

The three major German banks—Deutsche Bank, Commerzbank, and Dresdner Bank—were founded in the 1870s. Frankfurt remains the banking center of Germany and an international center of finance. The Frankfurt Stock Exchange is a leader in the world, and Frankfurt was chosen as the site for the EU's European Central Bank. Other exchanges can be found in Bremen, Düsseldorf, Hamburg, Munich, Hannover, Stuttgart, and Berlin.

Cargo ships line the docks of the harbor in Hamburg.

EAST AND WEST DISPARITIES

The economic challenges brought about by reunification have been great. Industries and businesses in the former East have not been able to remain competitive under capitalism, and many have closed. West German managerial skills have saved some industries, but the East German work force in general had fewer skills or motivational reasons for succeeding.

A government organization, the Treuhandanstalt, or Trust Agency, was set up to turn the entire East German economy into a free market economy. By 1994, the agency had turned approximately 14,000 formerly state-owned enterprises—98 percent of those entrusted to it—over to private hands. Hundreds of thousands of new businesses have opened and both western German and foreign firms, led by giants such as Siemens and General Motors, have set up shop in the former East Germany. In 1998 the eastern states were home to 520,000 small and medium-sized businesses with a total of 3.2 million employees. The number of self-employed easterners jumped in about ten years from 30,000 to 240,000.

The factory that produced the Trabant car (*above*) in the former East Germany went bankrupt after reunification as it could not compete against the more attractive vehicles of the West.

THE PROBLEMS OF REUNIFICATION The former East Germany had huge infrastructure costs to bear, as almost all its housing and commercial buildings were rundown and in need of repair. Public and private investment has done much to bring the East's basic infrastructure up to par with the West. Since 1990 over half a million new housing units have been built and 3.5 million existing residences have been renovated. Seven thousand miles (11,260 km) of roads and 3,000 miles (4,800 km) of rail lines have been rebuilt or newly constructed. The telecommunications system was completely replaced and now ranks among the most advanced in the world.

The currency unification, whereby former East Germans could exchange their money for West German notes, was completed in June 1991, though not without considerable loss of savings.

Much of the initial rejoicing over reunification disappeared as a whole host of problems—mainly social and economic—emerged. The government found that it was not easy bringing people who had been used to communist systems into capitalism. Some West German employers were quick to hire the most competent East German workers, taking away experienced people, particularly in health care and nursing, from the eastern states. Former West German workers felt their jobs were threatened by the flood of skilled and semiskilled workers from the East prepared to work for less money than their Western counterparts. Also, West Germans paid slightly higher taxes for one year in order to fund East German reconstruction.

WORKING LIFE

Germany has a powerful set of labor laws protecting workers' rights; laborers have a real say in the running of their work places by having a system of worker participation in management. Companies employing over 2,000 people have an *Aufsichtsrat* (OWF-sikts-raht), a council composed of delegates from workers and management. Firms with over five employees must have a *Beitriebsrat* (Bye-TREEBS-raht), a workers' council. These councils are consulted over recruitment, dismissals, unemployment, and new technology.

A motor worker on the production line

During the 1930s, the labor movement was divided into over 200 groups, making resistance to Nazism impossible. Today, there are 11 unions within the Deutscher Gewerkschaftsbund—the German Federation of Trade Unions. Roughly 38 percent of employees are unionized, with about 85–90 percent in the heavy industries.

Unions strive for better conditions, but fear of inflation keeps them from demanding excessive wages. Unions are arranged so that all workers in the same company belong to the same union, to avoid conflicts and duplicating negotiations. Once an annual wage agreement is signed, it is like a peace treaty and no strikes take place; during negotiations, a strike can take place only with the approval of a qualified majority of the workers voting by secret ballot. Only a union can call a strike.

Germans are generally hardworking, although reportedly less so than they used to be. They also have the shortest working year in the West after Belgium, with five to six weeks paid vacation and public holidays generally totaling more than 30 vacation days a year.

ENVIRONMENT

ENVIRONMENTAL ISSUES ARE EXTREMELY important in Germany. Germans make a conscious effort to protect the environment. This caring attitude toward the environment is the result of long-standing active public concern and participation, as well as progressive government policies and legislation that place strict limits on all forms of noise, water, air, and ground pollution. When the country was reunified in 1990, Germany had to reduce the dangerous pollution level in the former Eastern states caused by the toxic substances used in many of the former Eastern industries, in addition to protecting its existing national natural resources.

Above: **Factories line an inland harbor in the Ruhr industrial area.**

Opposite: **Quiet, scenic landscapes, like this one in Lake Tegern in the Alpine town of Bad Wiessee, provide soothing comfort to German city dwellers.**

Pollution prevention is only one facet of Germany's comprehensive approach to environmental conservation. The country is also very much committed to ensuring that recycling and the protection of natural resources are maximized in all spheres of human activity. This goal is achieved by several means—preventing pollution from entering the environment, promoting energy efficiency in the use of natural resources in the home and in industry, and halting and reversing the depletion of land and natural resources. As stated in Germany's Basic Law, the overall aim of environmental policies is to protect "vital natural resources on behalf of future generations."

As a result, the country is a leading producer of environmental technology and services aimed not only at eliminating pollution but also at developing renewable energy and protecting natural resources and the environment. This technical expertise is backed by some of Europe's most environmentally aware citizens, who are actively involved in protecting their natural heritage and scenic countryside.

A somber landscape in the Lüneburger Heath national park.

AIR POLLUTION

As one of the world's leading industrialized nations, Germany has come to terms with the impact that its heavy industrial activity and road traffic have had on the natural environment. Pollutants have caused great damage to Germany's atmosphere. Acid rain, which results from air pollution, eats away at the country's forests and lakes, destroying the natural habitat of wildlife. Acid rain also damages Germany's numerous historic buildings and town centers.

A far-reaching clean-air program has been implemented, targeting air pollution at its source. Measures have been taken to implement laws requiring car drivers, power stations, heavy industrial plants, and other polluting buildings or machinery to install catalytic converters, devices to treat exhaust gases before they are released into the air.

The government aims to reduce pollutants from traffic by banning the use of leaded gasoline and introducing tighter emissions standards for all classes of vehicles, regardless of whether they are road users or not, which means that aircraft are also affected. There is a concerted effort toward the creation of environmentally sustainable transportation by using new technology and educating the public on viable alternatives to fossil fuels.

The most visible signs of this changing mentality are probably the increasing appearance of buses that run on natural gas in urban centers across the country, as well as the promotion of bicycles as a healthy form of transportation on congested city roads.

Germany has worked to persuade its European partners to follow its lead in implementing creative environmental programs and has brought about the successful adoption of a standardized European Union-wide policy for clean fuels.

A city bus runs through Stuttgart.

The waters of the Elbe River run alongside the town of Magdeburg.

NOISE AND WATER POLLUTION

Germany has been active in reducing noise pollution across the country through the adoption and enforcement of strict noise control measures, especially in urban residential areas. The government has taken the first step by reducing traffic as well as controlling noise from cars and other vehicles. The Blue Angel "environment-friendly" label, in use since 1977, has helped to raise awareness of all pollution issues, including noise, among the general public. This label, although not legally binding, is sought after by manufacturers because of the sales boost it gives a product that is recognized as environmentally friendly.

Water pollution issues are often international, as rivers cross borders. Germany has been working closely with its neighbors to remedy water pollution issues and has contributed handsomely to clean-up measures abroad. Germany and its neighbors have signed cooperation agreements concerning the protection of the Danube, Oder, and Elbe rivers.

Levels of water pollution from Germany's industrial centers have also improved over the last decade as a result of tougher legislation on industrial waste water disposal. The levels of lead in the Rhine river have decreased by half. Nitrate levels in the waterways caused by run-offs of agricultural chemicals have fallen as well.

Germany's efforts do not aim to simply reduce the existing level of water pollution, but also to remedy past abuses to the environment and rehabilitate once-choked waterways into clean, ecologically viable habitats not only for people, but for the many species of wildlife to be found there.

FLOOD PREVENTION

Disastrous floods have hit Germany in recent years. The most recent, and, according to many, the worst flood in the history of Germany took place in August 2002. The Elbe river, swollen by heavy rains, burst its banks, causing massive damage to towns and cities along its course.

The government has put a great deal of effort into alleviating the effects—both human and economic—of past floods, and is working to prevent similar catastrophes from recurring. Measures to remedy the effects of floods, beyond the already existing work to ensure clear paths for Germany's waterways, have included identifying and shielding damage-prone flood plains, as well as improvement of area capabilities for retention and absorption of precipitation.

A THW (Technical Assistance Service) worker wades his way through the flood waters that cover the courtyard of the famous Zwinger castle in Dresden in August 2002. The floods caused by the overflowing waters of the Elbe river have been the worst in German history.

German citizens must separate and dispose of garbage according to strict regulations. Color-coded bins, like these in Düsseldorf, are used for collecting different types of recyclable waste.

RECYCLING

Germany takes the world lead in recycling—over 30 percent of domestic waste is recycled, more than in any other developed country. The widespread use of glass instead of plastic containers and the rapid growth of comprehensive recycling facilities bear testimony to the determination and commitment the government has put into this initiative, as well as to the efficiency with which it has implemented the program nationwide.

The country's recycling-friendly Green Dot scheme is known worldwide, and, thanks to Germany's phenomenal export success, consumer items bearing the scheme's logo can be seen on shop shelves around the globe. The Green Dot "polluter pays" campaign, by which producers must ensure the proper disposal of the packaging of their products, has recently been joined by new recycling requirements for end-consumers, requiring them to pay a deposit on various types of containers, refundable on the return of these to designated outlets. Unlike the Blue Angel scheme, the newer plans are designed to ensure that everyone has an economic stake in re-using packaging.

AN END TO NUCLEAR POWER

Despite expressed public desire to continue the use of nuclear power, the German government has committed itself to ending its use by the mid-2020s as a matter of environmental principle. This is a momentous decision considering that Germany is reliant on the 19 nuclear power stations currently in use for approximately 30 percent of its total electricity needs.

The negotiations leading to this breakthrough have been lengthy and compromising continues, most recently with the delayed closure of Germany's oldest operating pressurised water reactor plant (Obrigheim, dating from 1969), now to be axed in 2005, two years later than planned. The transport and processing of radioactive waste was put on hold for four years because of safety issues. However, shipment of radioactive waste to processing facilities in La Hague, France, and Sellafield, United Kingdom has resumed. The processed waste will eventually be returned to Germany for final storage underground a former salt mine near the village of Gorleben. Meanwhile, spent fuel rods from operating plants are also required to be stored in interim depots near the plants themselves before final disposal.

THE WAY FORWARD

The impressive steps that Germany has taken over the last 40 years in environmental protection and pollution minimization does not mean, however, that there is nothing left to be done. There remain continuing challenges in all areas of pollution control, further steps in integrating environmental concerns into economic decisions, and continuing international environmental cooperation. But the energy and determination with which the government and the German people have proceeded to protect their natural environment and resources in the past is a good sign that the country will maintain its present lead as one of the world's standard bearers for economically viable environmental protection.

A nuclear power station in Gundremmingen, Bavaria.

DREHORGEL — PAULE

GERMANS

MORE THAN 83 MILLION PEOPLE LIVE IN GERMANY. Although Germany is currently the most populous nation in the EU, it has one of the lowest birth rates in the world; it is estimated that only 1.4 children are born to the average couple. This decline in the birth rate is expected to continue, as more German couples marry later in life or choose not to have children.

The majority of Germans live in the huge conurbations (continuous networks of urban communities) of the Rhine-Ruhr valley near Cologne, the Rhine-Main area near Frankfurt, and the Swabian industrial area near Stuttgart, where jobs and recreational facilities are more plentiful.

One in three Germans lives in a large city, and about 80 percent of the total population lives in cities with a population of 100,000 or more.

Left: **Germans relaxing in a square in Munich.**

Opposite: **An organ grinder in Bavaria.**

Crowds gather at Alexanderplatz in Berlin.

GERMAN CHARACTERISTICS

The German nation grew from the different tribes of Franks, Saxons, Bavarians, and Swabians, and these continue to be active regional groups. Although the influx of thousands of immigrants has influenced the German character, some stereotypes persist. Rhinelanders are thought to be easygoing, and Swabians thrifty. Those from south Germany, particularly Bavaria, are thought of as politically conservative and generally Roman Catholic; those from the north are expected to be Protestant and liberal. Berliners and people from the province of Schleswig-Holstein have a reputation for being talkative.

Germans have a love for bureaucracy, and most people obey and rarely question rules. A love of order translates into extreme neatness, and families are often very proud of their homes.

Perhaps due to their bitter experiences during the Nazi regime, Germans in general do not openly express feelings of national patriotism, preferring to pledge their loyalties to their hometown or region.

THE WITTELSBACHS

The Wittelsbach family ruled Bavaria from 1180 to 1918, first as dukes and later as monarchs. After World War I, Ludwig III formally gave up the throne, and the family gave several castles, including Neuschwanstein and Linderhoff (*below*), and works of art to the state of Bavaria. The family still owns the Hohenschwangen castle near Neuschwanstein, which is used as a retreat.

During the Nazi period in the 1930s and 1940s, the Wittelsbach family, led by Ludwig III's son, Prince Rupert, opposed and resisted Adolf Hitler by producing an opposition newspaper. As a result, many family members were sent to concentration camps between 1944 and 1945, spending the last days of the war in Dachau concentration camp until they were liberated by the American army.

Today, the family still makes use of the Nymphenburg palace in Bavaria for particular functions. Prince Rupert's son, Albert the Duke of Bavaria, played a visible role in Bavarian society until his death in 1996 at the age of 91. In 1980, when Pope John Paul II visited Bavaria, Albert was among those who greeted him.

Some people in Bavaria still call the current duke, Franz, "your royal highness." The Wittelsbach family remains popular in the region, they are closely identified with local traditions and heritage, and remembered as good and kind rulers.

A Bavarian in traditional clothing wears the typical green felt hat decorated with feathers.

DRESS

For everyday wear, Germans choose jeans, T-shirts or sweatshirts, leather jackets, and sneakers or leather shoes. Large cities such as Berlin, Hamburg, Munich, Frankfurt, and Düsseldorf have an array of local and international boutiques with designer clothing for the fashion-conscious. Although German dress is becoming more casual on the whole, it is still acceptable to dress in full evening dress—long dresses for women, tuxedos or tails for men—when attending formal functions such as the opera or theater performances, as well as high-class clubs and casinos.

Dress variations do exist between the regions, although traditional outfits are now worn mostly during festivals. Visible examples are the Baltic Sea blue jacket and trousers with a peaked cap, the Hamburg blue sailor's cap, or the Bavarian *dirndl* (DURN-dil) dress and apron. The famous short leather trousers, called *lederhosen* (LAY-der-HO-zen) are found throughout Germany.

The traditional Munich-style dress is the Bavarian *Tracht* (TRAHCT) or *loden* (LOH-den): green wool capes and jackets. Instead of *lederhosen*, Bavarian men might wear grey or green trousers with a waterproof woven jacket and a green felt hat topped by a pair of feathers. These costumes are worn during festive occasions, more often in rural than urban areas.

The immigrant Turkish community can be easily identified by its conservatively dressed women, who generally wear scarves rather than the full head coverings worn by Muslim women in the Middle East.

IMMIGRANTS AND MINORITIES

Today, about 7.5 million people living in Germany are non-German citizens. The Turks, who number about 2 million, are the largest group of foreigners. During the period of the "economic miracle" of the 1950s and 1960s, German factories had a shortage of blue-collar labor. The German and Turkish governments signed an agreement to enable Turks to work in Germany as *Gastarbeiter* (GAST-ahr-byte er), or "guest workers." The Turks have since built their own close-knit communities in Germany. Berlin is the city with the largest Turkish population outside of Turkey.

Other immigrant communities include former Yugoslavs (estimated to number about 1 million, including many war refugees), Italians (565,000), Greeks (350,000), Poles (260,000), and Austrians (185,000), as well as smaller numbers of Russians, Romanians, Spaniards, Africans, and Asians.

German reunification has brought about unemployment among the minority groups, as an abundant supply of labor from the eastern states poses competition for jobs that were usually performed by immigrants.

Minority students with their classmates in a lecture hall at the University of Rostock.

67

MINORITIES The group that is not represented in large numbers are the Jews. Before 1933, there were about 600,000 Jews in Germany; after World War II, barely 25,000 remained. The consequent loss of creative talent, entrepreneurship, and cultural achievement cannot be measured. Dachau Concentration Camp, where thousands of Jews were murdered by the Nazis, is the fourth most visited site in Germany today. There are about 50,000 Jews in present-day Germany, but they are mostly the descendants of Jewish refugees who fled the Soviet Union after World War II.

About 60,000 Sorbians, a Slavic minority, live between the Oder and Neisse rivers. Road signs in this region are in both Sorb and German. There is also a small Frisian-speaking minority on the North Sea coast.

Today, immigrant and minority workers have considerable political rights within Germany. In addition, they can enjoy comprehensive health, education, and welfare benefits. However, some restrictions to full integration into German society still apply. German immigration laws, for instance, do not allow foreigners to become German citizens, unless they can trace their background to German ancestors. And, although not as pervasive as the mass media reports, xenophobic attacks by Neo-Nazis in Germany numbered 14,000 in 2000, a 14 percent increase from the previous year.

CLASS DIVISIONS

The German aristocracy played a dominant role in society until 1918. They have been replaced by an industrial class of wealthy manufacturers and business people, who prospered in former West Germany in the years following the end of World War II. In keeping with the traditional German values of modesty and frugality, this new class, in general, dislikes displaying its wealth in an extravagant manner.

Nevertheless, some traces of the old aristocracy still remain. Romantic castles built by the old aristocrats abound in Germany, and Germans whose last name begins with *von* (FOHN) can trace their ancestry to the old aristocracy. Present-day German aristocrats have retained a few priviliges, such as private ownership of some small-scale castles. They generally regard their position in life as a privilege and many are involved in social and charity work.

Opposite: **A Turkish Immigrant lady and her child take a rest in a public square in Germany.**

Below: **A shepherd and his sheepdog tend a flock near the Elbe River.**

The upper middle class is made up of managers, professionals, and civil servants, while the lower class has decreased as more and more people have attained the education, income, and lifestyle of the middle class. The prevailing German public lifestyle is that of the lower middle class.

Social divisions today are based on wealth. And differences among Germans are between the employed and the unemployed, and former East and West Germans.

LIFESTYLE

MOST GERMANS SPEND THEIR WORK and leisure time in the same ways as people in other Western countries. Families are generally small and nuclear, consisting of only father, mother, and one or two children, particularly in urban areas.

Often, both parents work in order to keep up with the high cost of living. Young people dress casually in jeans and T-shirts. American culture is very influential in Germany, and American sitcoms, sports events, and popular music are closely followed by the young.

Within Germany, there remain great variations in lifestyle—between the urban and the rural, the different localities, the employed and the unemployed, the former East and West Germans.

Left: **German luxury cars line a fashionable street in Munich.**

Opposite: **Originally found in French cities, outdoor cafés have become a part of life in present-day Germany.**

Gabled houses and shops line the historic Market Place in Bremen.

HOUSING

Many Germans dream of owning a house with a garden. About 40 percent of Germans living in the western states own their own homes, which generally come with all modern conveniences. Seventy percent of housing in the western states has been built since 1945. Rent and mortgage payments make up a high proportion of a family's monthly expenses.

Architectural styles vary throughout Germany, depending on local building materials and the climate. In the Alpine area, chalet-style houses are built on south-facing slopes. In North-Rhine Westphalia, half-timbered houses have slates covering their western walls for protection against the biting wind. Some city residential areas offer restored 19th century blocks of buildings for sale or rental; high-rise blocks with basic facilities are available for lower-income families in some suburban areas.

FAMILY LIFE

In urban areas both spouses must work in order to be able to afford the contemporary German's ideal lifestyle—home ownership and overseas holidays. The size of the German family is decreasing; on average, a family has just one or two children. In the rural areas of southern Germany, families with several generations living under the same roof can be found, but this is rare in urban areas. The population mainly consists of families with unmarried children (57 percent) or of married couples who are childless or no longer have children living in at home (23 percent).

People are relatively free to marry whom they choose, and marriage is no longer the only option: 40 percent of couples between the ages of 18 and 35 live together without being legally married. Children of unmarried parents have the same legal rights as children of traditional marriages.

Family and friends gather in a beer and wine garden in the Rhine valley town of Boppard.

CHILDHOOD RITUALS

Babies are christened or baptized soon after their birth, regardless of whether they come from a Protestant or Catholic family. For Catholics, the child's first communion at the age of seven is an important event; for Protestants, confirmation at around 14 is a major occasion. However, in present-day secular society, the first day at school is replacing religious rituals as the most important occasion in a child's life.

YOUTH

Just 15 percent of the population is under 14. In order to encourage couples to have children, tax breaks are given for each child. In addition, a child's education is free from elementary school to university. Many laws protect the rights of children, thus child pornography is strictly prohibited. As in many modern westernized societies, despite their material wealth, drug addiction is a problem for some young people in urban areas.

WEDDINGS

During the engagement period, German couples wear a gold ring on the fourth finger of the left hand. In order to be legally married couples must go through a civil ceremony in a registry office (often in the town hall). Family and friends gather outside the town hall to throw rice and flowers at the newlyweds as they emerge from the town hall. Only the civil marriage is considered legal in Germany.

The church wedding, generally on the weekend after the civil ceremony, is optional but still popular with couples who belong to a church and pay church taxes. During the religious ceremony small page boys and flower girls enter the church followed by the bride and groom. The gold engagement rings are moved from the left to the right hand of both the bride and groom during the service. After the ceremony there is usually a reception for family and friends, with food and drinks, speeches, and dancing. The 25th and 50th wedding anniversaries are family celebrations.

A couple arrives at their wedding the old-fashioned way—by horse and carriage.

DEATHS

Deaths are announced in the newspapers. Relatives send black-rimmed notifications of the funeral arrangements to friends and acquaintances.

Funerals are a time of family reunion where support is given to the deceased's family. German families rarely hold full wakes these days; wakes are mostly confined to small, conservative Catholic towns. Calla lilies, tall white flowers, are the traditional flowers for funeral services.

It is customary for the surviving partner to wear both wedding rings as a sign of widowhood. Graves are tended regularly, and full mourning dress (black clothes) can be worn.

A cross commemorating an East German who was shot while trying to escape to the West.

WOMEN

According to the Basic Law, women enjoy the same legal rights as men; in actual employment, however, inequalities do exist. Within marriage, laws protect women's property rights. Husband and wife can take either the woman's or the man's last name, keep their own names, or choose both names—a *doppelname* (DOH-pull NAH-meh)—without adding a hyphen.

In the case of divorce, the wealthier partner continues to support the other regardless of who is responsible for the breakup of the marriage.

Women employees are more likely to become unemployed during a recession, and fewer are promoted into top posts. Male employees still receive higher wages than their female counterparts. Most of the political parties have introduced quotas to increase the number of female representatives on executive committees. The CDU and the Green Party have female leaders. In the current government, seven of the 15 federal ministers are women.

A teacher conducting a class. About 55 percent of German women between the ages of 15 and 65 are employed. The high cost of child care is one of the reasons why many German women choose not to work. In the former East Germany, child care was provided by the state, enabling over 80 percent of women to join the work force.

A busy shopping arcade
in Potsdam Platz, Berlin.

SHOPPING

Large supermarkets and shopping centers are located in the center of most German cities. Most shops close at 6:30 P.M. on weekdays and 2 P.M. on Saturdays; some shops stay open until 8 P.M. on weekdays and 4 P.M. on Saturdays. The first Saturday of every month is known as *langer Samstag* (LAHNG-ur SAHMS-tahg) or "long Saturday," when shops close at 6 P.M. All shops are closed on Sundays, following the 1956 Shop Closure Law.

EDUCATION

Education is compulsory for children from the age of 6 to 18. The school year runs from the end of August to June or July, with a half-year assessment report in February. There is a six-week summer holiday and two weeks' vacation during Christmas and Easter. The length and time of the holidays differ from state to state. The school day lasts from 8 A.M. to 1 P.M., Monday through Friday, and from 8 A.M. to noon on Saturday. School

hours are devoted almost completely to academic subjects, with few nonacademic activities. Children return home for lunch after school and spend the afternoon doing their homework.

German children begin elementary school—*Grundschule* (GROONT-shoo-leh)—at the age of 6. Elementary school lasts from four to five years, depending on the state. At around the age of 10, children must choose between three types of schools: *Hauptschule* (HOWPT-shoo-leh), *Realschule* (RAY-ahl-shoo-leh), and *Gymnasium* (ghim-NAH-zee-um).

About one-half of the children progress to *Hauptschule*, where they continue to receive full-time general education until the age of 15 or 16. After *Hauptschule*, pupils proceed to a part-time vocational school. About one-third of the students proceed to *Realschule*, where they receive a comprehensive general education. A *Realschule* certificate qualifies students to proceed to a technical school. Less than one-fourth of children proceed to *Gymnasium* , which prepares students to take the *Abitur* (AH-bee-toor) exam after nine years of study, a requirement to enter university.

Medical students at the Humboldt University in Berlin. Roughly 1.8 million students are enrolled in German universities, and 153,000 of them are foreigners.

TYPES OF SCHOOL AND FURTHER EDUCATION Most German children attend state schools; about 10 percent attend private schools—usually run by churches, and 13 percent attend the popular Free Waldorf schools, where equal emphasis is placed on both academic and artistic subjects. Each state runs its own education system and appoints teachers; however, teachers are subject to the authority of the Federal Ministry of Education.

German universities have a long tradition of academic excellence. However, the large number of applicants has resulted in overcrowded school facilities. Student places are usually awarded on the basis of the applicant's *Abitur* grade average. Courses of study in new technological fields have been introduced to keep pace with current industrial trends. University courses culminate in either a *Magister* (MAH-ghee-steh) or *Diplom* (DIH-plohm) examination or a state examination.

University education is free of charge at present, but the economic downturn has sparked a debate on whether students should be made to pay their own tuition fees.

HEALTH CARE

Health care in Germany is well funded and equipped, providing health insurance for all employees, the self-employed, and their dependents, regardless of their nationality. The lower income groups and the unemployed are provided for by state and federal projects. Still, occasional abuses to the system are reported.

There are about 282,700 doctors in Germany. They work in private practice or in one of the 2,040 general hospitals (831 public hospitals, 835 maintained by independent or non-profit organizations, 374 private hospitals).

A physician attending to an elderly patient.

RELIGION

GERMANY IS A SECULAR STATE, with freedom of religion guaranteed by the Basic Law. All registered members of large Christian denominations—Roman Catholic, Calvinist, Lutheran—and Jewish synagogues must pay a church tax.

More than 56 million people in Germany (68 percent of the population) belong to a Christian church—28.2 million are Protestant and 28.2 million are Roman Catholic. Although only a small percentage of German Christians attend church on Sundays, Sunday is still regarded as a day of rest in Germany. Most shops are closed and there are strict rules about performing any type of work on Sundays.

The former East Germany had no religious instruction in school, and socialist rites replaced religious ceremonies at birth, marriage, and death.

The *Jugendweihe* (YOO-gund-vye-eh) was established by the government in the 1950s as a secular coming-of-age ritual meant to replace the rite of confirmation in Christian churches. Sociologists have observed that many eastern Germans, 10 years after reunification, are experiencing *Ostalgie* (OHST-ahl-ghee), defined as "eastern nostalgia," and developing a distinct eastern identity rooted in the experience of life in the former GDR. As a result, the *Jugendweihe*, which briefly fell out of fashion after unification, has regained popularity among eastern teenagers and their parents.

Above: **A sculpture of saints and angels on the corner of a building in Bamberg, Bavaria.**

Opposite: **The gorgeous interior of the Birnau Pilgrimage Church. Built in the 1700s, it is located near Lake Constance.**

German Christians pack a church during an evangelical meeting in Berlin.

CHURCH IN SOCIETY

Many leading members of the Protestant and Catholic churches stood up against Adolf Hitler during World War II and, as a result, the churches see themselves as protectors of freedom and democracy. This proved to be true again in 1989 when church members played a big part in the downfall of former communist East Germany and the re-emergence of democracy in that part of the country.

Both Protestant and Catholic churches run a variety of social services—schools, kindergartens, nursing homes, programs for the disabled, hospitals, and other organizations—that fill a general social need and are offered to people of all religious backgrounds.

The country is broadly divided between a mainly Protestant north and a Catholic south. However, the large influx of refugees from Eastern Europe in 1945, as well as East Germans during the 1940s and 1950s, has served to blur these lines and give more communities a truly mixed Christian population.

CATHOLICISM

The predominantly Catholic areas of Germany have traditionally been the Rhineland-Palatinate, Saarland, and Bavaria, with an equal number of Catholics and Protestants in Baden-Württemberg and North Rhine-Westphalia. The Catholic Church in Germany consists of five church provinces with five archbishoprics—Cologne, Paderborn, Munich, Bamberg and Freiburg, and Berlin—and 22 bishoprics. The colorful festivals of Corpus Christi and Ascension Day are celebrated in Catholic areas.

PROTESTANTISM

Protestants in Germany for the most part belong to three denominations: Lutheran, Reformed (Calvinist or Zwinglian), and United (a combination of Reformed and Lutheran). Protestantism is practiced predominantly in the north. Churches are grouped into an alliance of 24 mostly independent churches known as the *Evangelische Kirche in Deutschland* (ehh-vahn-GHEL-ish-eh KEER-kheh een DOYTCH-lahnd), or EKD, at the top of which is a synod for legislative matters and a council for executive matters. Most Lutheran churches are also grouped into the United Evangelical Lutheran Church of Germany, or the VELKD.

Inside the solemn Cologne cathedral.

There are also "free" churches, which are affiliated with smaller Protestant denominations such as Baptists and Pentecostals. The Methodists and the Evangelical community have joined to become the Evangelical Methodist Church. There are small numbers of Quakers, Mennonites, and the Salvation Army, well known for their social and educational work.

MARTIN LUTHER

It was in Germany that Christianity first split into Roman Catholicism and Protestantism. In 1517, Martin Luther, an Augustinian monk, criticized the Catholic Church for selling "indulgences" as a means of fund-raising. An indulgence was the temporary forgiveness of sins before the final absolution was granted after confession. The money raised from the selling of indulgences funded the building of such beautiful and imposing churches as St. Peter's Church in Rome. Corruption was common among church leaders of the time. Luther argued for equality between layperson and priest, disputed the Pope's authority and the role of the clergy, and asserted the individual's right to read the Scriptures for himself or herself, translating the Bible from Greek to German to help people do so.

Luther's moral protest was adopted for political ends by a number of German princes. His protest against the Church's abuse of authority indirectly triggered off the Peasants' Revolt in 1524, which was forcibly put down by the princes. Religious wars in the 16th and 17th centuries killed many Germans and reduced the country to a series of tiny states.

OTHER BELIEFS

JUDAISM The Jewish population in Germany before 1933 was about 600,000, but the horrors of the Holocaust and emigration have reduced that number to around 50,000 today. There are Jewish congregations throughout Germany, the largest are in Berlin and Frankfurt, Germany's banking center which was largely started by Jews. Acts of atonement have been performed by former German leaders at Israel's monuments to the war, and reparations were agreed upon and paid to Israel during the 1970s. The reluctance of large numbers of Jews to return to Germany has deprived the country of much creative talent. Recently, anti-Semitism has resurfaced in some areas of the country, particularly in the eastern states.

ISLAM The large Turkish minority mainly centered in Berlin makes up the bulk of Germany's Muslims. It is estimated that about 3 million Muslims from 41 nations live in Germany. Rights of worship, education, and religious schooling are all guaranteed under German law. German employers often set aside rooms to allow Muslim employees to carry out their daily prayers. The Muslim festival of Ramadan and observances and arrangements for the pilgrimage to Mecca are all carried out with the help of religious leaders and government bodies. The government works with Turkey to bring religious teachers to Germany to preach to its Turkish minority. Liberal rather than fundamentalist preachers are preferred, so that the Turks will have fewer problems integrating into German society.

ATHEISM A significant proportion of German youth are either atheist or simply uninterested in religion. This is common in urban centers, especially Berlin, and in the former East Germany, where atheism was encouraged and taught, even though religious freedom was allowed.

Although Germany is a secular state, Christianity still has a great effect on culture, personal attitudes, social structure, and even politics. One of the ruling political parties, the Christian Democratic Union, is strongly supported by Catholics and Protestants.

LANGUAGE

GERMAN IS SPOKEN THROUGHOUT GERMANY and in parts of neighboring Luxembourg, Switzerland, the Netherlands, Italy, and Austria. This common language was a uniting force among the people long before Germany became a nation, and remains a common bond between states and regions today. The language is changing, with increasing additions from other Western languages, particularly American and British English.

Together with German, Frisian is spoken along the North Sea coast; Danish just along the frontier with Denmark in Schleswig-Holstein; and Slavonic Sorbian in parts of Lusatia, Berlin, and east of the Elbe River. Many Germans speak English fluently and many former East Germans can converse in Russian.

Left: **"The wall must go," says the graffiti on the Berlin Wall.**

Opposite: **Two men read the news. Germans are avid newspaper readers.**

The Gutenberg Bible, dating from the 1460s, is one of Germany's first printed books.

THE GERMAN LANGUAGE

As the English language has Germanic roots, many German words are similar to English words, both in meaning and pronunciation: *gut* (good), *Buch* (book), *fein* (fine), *Haus* (house), *Preis* (price). Perhaps the most peculiar characteristic about German is the length of some words. These are generally compound words, which explain a combined meaning that could easily take a whole phrase in English to translate. Several German words have crept into the English language, for example, kindergarten, wanderlust, rucksack, hinterland, and leitmotif.

German grammar can seem overwhelmingly complicated to English speakers. The language uses three different genders (neuter, male, and female) and four different cases (nominative, dative, accusative, and genitive). Each noun starts with a capital letter, and any qualifying adjectives agree in gender and case with the noun. German word order is quite unlike English, with the verb falling at the end of the sentence rather than immediately after the subject.

SCRIPT

If you look at written German, you may come across a curious sign, ß, nowadays written as "ss," which is pronounced "tz." Another is a letter that resembles an "f," but is in fact the way an "s" is written at the beginning of a word. Both characters are no longer commonly used in today's newspapers. Several German newspapers use versions of the old German script for their title letterings. Original works by Goethe and Schiller written in this old style are almost unrecognizable today.

PRONUNCIATION

Pronunciation is generally straightforward, with the stress on the root of a word, often the first syllable. Consonants are broadly pronounced as in English, though some combinations differ. These are listed below.

Letter	Example	Pronunciation
ch	*acht*	guttural "ch" as in Scottish "loch"
chs	*sechs*	"ks" as in "wakes"
d	*und*	"t" as in "wait" at the end of a word, otherwise as in English
pf	*Pferd*	"pf"—the "p" is pronounced subtly
qu	*Qualität*	"kkv"—no equivalent in English
s	*Sie*	"z" as in "zoo" at the beginning of a word, otherwise as in English
v	*Vögel*	"f" as in "full" at the beginning of a word, otherwise as in English
w	*Wir*	"v" as in "vex"

One reason why foreigners find it hard to understand German is that a number of words are compounds of smaller words. Different nouns can be joined, such as Rathaus, *which is a compound of* Rat *(parliament) and* Haus *(house). So the compound* Rathaus *means the building where parliament meets.*

About 10 percent of all books published throughout the world have been written in German. Also, more works have been translated into German than into any other language.

Vowels and vowel combinations are pronounced differently from English, although they generally follow the rules below.

Letter	Example	Pronunciation
a	*Land*	short "a" as in "hat"
a	*Name*	soft "a" as in "father"
ä	*Länder*	"e" sound as in "lender"
ai	*Kaiser*	long "i" as in "height"
au	*Haus*	"ow" as in "house"
äu	*Häuser*	"oy" as in "soil"
e	*Sechs*	short "e" as in "set"
e	*dritte*	unstressed, like "e" in "open"
ee	*Nordsee*	"ay" as in "say"
ei	*weiss*	long "i" as in "white"
eu	*euch*	"oy" as in "soil"
i	*Ich*	short "i" as in "in"
ie	*Sie*	"ee" sound as in "tea"
o	*wo*	long "o" as in "woe"
o	*Doppel*	short "o" as in "on"
ö	*Löffel*	"er" as in "berth"
u	*Buch*	"oo" as in "boot"
ü	*Bücher*	fine "u," like "unique" without the "y" sound

As the table shows, vowels with *umlauts* (two dots over letters—pronounced OOM-louts) are pronounced differently from those without. When publishers are unable to set *umlauts*, an extra "e" is added to indicate altered pronunciation (and often meaning). For instance, *Bücher* can be written as *Buecher*.

HIGH AND LOW GERMAN

High German is German that is traditionally spoken in southern and central Germany—the regions with the higher terrain—and is now accepted and taught as the standard language. By contrast, Low German is the language spoken on the low, flat northern plain.

The main difference between the two languages was caused by the German Sound Shift, which occurred between the 5th and 8th centuries, whereby the consonants "p," "t," and "k" became "f" or "pf"; "ss" or "z"; and "ch," respectively. Thus:

Low German	*Slapen*	*Appel*	*Water*	*Tid*	*Maken*
High German	*Schlafen*	*Apfel*	*Wasser*	*Zeit*	*Machen*
English	Sleep	Apple	Water	Time	Make

Unlike people from Mediterranean cultures, Germans tend to use little facial expression when speaking to one another.

FORMS OF ADDRESS

In Germany there are different ways of addressing people, depending on how well you know them, their social or professional status, whether they are older or younger than you, and so on. The most polite word for "you," in both the singular and plural form, is *Sie* (zee), which Germans use in direct address until they become familiar with the person that they are speaking with. It is similar in English to calling someone Mr. or Mrs. until they invite you to call them by their first name.

However, it would not be considered unusual, or rude, to continue addressing business associates in a long-term working relationship using the formal *Sie*. First names are rarely heard in offices. *Herr* (HAIR) or *Frau* (FROW) so-and-so remains the usual form of address at work, particularly among older people. A gulf separates one's office and private life.

Close friends, siblings, and young people in general use the informal *du* (DOO) to address one another. Parents use *du* when talking to their children. University students use *du* regardless of age differences but not before asking, "Can we call each other *du?*"

A lawyer, doctor, or professor should be addressed with a professional title, for example, *Frau Doktor* or *Herr Professor*. Old aristocratic families can be recognized by the *von* in the surname, as in Maria von Döhnhoff, former publisher of the weekly *Die Zeit*.

BODY LANGUAGE AND ETIQUETTE

Social interaction is often quite formal in Germany. People shake hands when introduced or when greeting people they already know, and are protective of their personal space and privacy. At mealtimes it is impolite to start eating before your host has wished you *Guten Appetit* (GOOT-en ahp-eh-TEET).

THE MEDIA

Germany has 370 daily newspapers (*above*), almost all regional, which combined have a circulation of 25.2 million copies a day. There are constitutional safeguards against any kind of censorship—although papers do sometimes reflect the interest of their owners.

Freedom of speech is guaranteed in the Basic Law—with the exception of Nazi propaganda, which is strictly prohibited by law. Freedom of speech, however, sometimes unwittingly allows the practice of scandalmongering by various newspapers. Thus these newspapers' use of scandalous news to woo readers is seldom punished.

Among the largest circulation papers are *Die Welt* and the *Suddeutsche Zeitung*, both on the political right; the *Frankfurter Allgemeine Zeitung* , which has a liberal slant; and the *Bild Zeitung*, the daily tabloid with sensational scoop stories and a circulation of 4.4 million. The Axel Springer Group, one of the largest publishing empires in Europe, publishes periodicals and newspapers.

ARTS

OVER THE CENTURIES, Germany has been the cradle of European music, literature, theater, and fine arts. From Beethoven and Bach to Goethe, Heine, and Schiller, Germany has produced some of the finest musicians and writers in the history of the civilized world. A strong cultural tradition remains in present-day Germany, and local musical and theatrical performances are always well patronized.

MUSIC

Germans are passionately fond of music, poetry, and drama. Almost every town is Germany has a small theater or opera house, its own amateur troupe, an orchestra or small musical group, and maybe a choral society. Music and singing play a big part in social activities and public celebrations.

Above: **The state opera house in Dresden's Theaterplatz.**

Opposite: **A gigantic sculpture of a "walking man" adorns the entrance of the Münchener Rück building, an insurance company in Munich.**

Germany has 141 professional orchestras, including famous ones such as the Berlin Philharmonic Orchestra, the Munich Philharmonic Orchestra, and the Bamberg Symphonic Orchestra. There are 121 government-subsidized opera houses and concert halls, of which Hamburg's (founded in 1678) is the oldest, as well as 1,000 theaters and 3,000 museums.

Classical recordings under famous conductors such as Herbert von Karajan have sold in the millions worldwide. Radio orchestras reach out to those who are unable to attend live performances. Artistic festivals occur frequently, celebrating famous local composers, playwrights, or performers.

Music education is strongly supported by the government. Conservatories, music colleges, and youth councils encourage young people to develop their talents in performing, as well as in listening to, all types of music. Local choral groups and quartets are active throughout the country.

GREAT MUSICIANS

Music, like language, knows no boundaries, and composers based in Austria, such as Wolfgang Amadeus Mozart, Christoph Gluck, and Franz Haydn, are often regarded as part of German musical culture.

Johann Sebastian Bach (1685–1750) was born in Eisenach, Thuringia, and worked as a choir director in Leipzig for much of his life. He composed organ pieces and orchestral works in the baroque style. His works include the *Brandenburg Concertos* and church music like the *St. Matthew Passion*.

George Frideric Händel (1685–1759) traveled widely in Italy and England. He composed operas and the famous oratorio, *The Messiah*, and the orchestral suites *The Water Music* and *Music for the Royal Fireworks*.

Ludwig van Beethoven (1770–1827) was born in Bonn and studied under Haydn and Mozart in Vienna. A prolific composer, his works include 32 piano sonatas, five piano concertos, nine symphonies, 17 string quartets, one opera (*Fidelio*), and numerous overtures. He became deaf at the age of 30 and was thus unable to hear many of his works performed.

Felix Mendelssohn (1809–1847), a successor of Beethoven, traveled widely in Britain and Italy. He composed the overture *Fingal's Cave* and the *Fourth "Italian" Symphony*. Robert Schumann (1810–1856) composed numerous piano pieces and chamber music, as well as four symphonies. Richard Wagner (1813–1883) intensified the emotional content of the Romantic style in his numerous operas. Johannes Brahms (1833–1897) developed a classic Romantic style in his symphonies, piano concertos, and other works.

Richard Strauss (1864–1949) wrote operas that include *Der Rosenkavalier* and many instrumental pieces. Paul Hindemith (1895–1963) composed post-Romantic instrumental music. Carl Orff (1895–1982) wrote operas and dramatic works, such as *Carmina Burana*, based on a 13th-century

collection of Bavarian songs. Two other influential German composers are Hans Werner Henze (b. 1926) and Karlheinz Stockhausen (b. 1928).

A group of students performs classical music for passers-by in Bavaria.

BEETHOVEN'S SYMPHONIES A radical departure from previous musical styles, these works celebrated emotion and developed themes at length.

The Third Symphony was at first dedicated to Napoleon Bonaparte but was altered when the leader's violent and cruel nature became apparent to Beethoven. It was renamed the *Sinfonia Eroica*, or heroic symphony.

The Fifth Symphony, or *Victory Symphony*, has one of the most famous openings in all of music: three short notes followed by a long one.

The Sixth Symphony, or *Pastoral Symphony*, has a rural theme and opens with a springlike awakening in which bird songs can be heard.

The Ninth "Choral" Symphony contains the rousing setting of Schiller's *Ode to Joy* in its final choral movement.

THE BAYREUTH FESTIVAL

In 1864, after years of financial difficulties and strong controversy surrounding his works, German writer and composer Richard Wagner won the support of the young king of Bavaria, Ludwig II, a fervent admirer of Wagner and his works. The king set Wagner and his family up in a villa in the small Bavarian town of Bayreuth, which Wagner named Wahnfried, which means "peace from illusion." Today, the villa houses a museum dedicated to Wagner's life and works.

Thanks to the full support and sponsorship of the king, Wagner was able to fulfill his life-long dream of building an opera house dedicated to German music and composers. In 1876, the Festspielhaus was completed and it opened with Wagner's *The Ring Cycle* operas, which consist of *Rhinegold*, *The Valkyrie*, *Siegfried*, and *The Twilight of the Gods*. In 1882, Wagner's last work, the *Parsifal* opera, was premiered at the Festspielhaus.

Since then, the Festspielhaus has been holding the Richard Wagner Festival every summer, closing only during the two World Wars. Today the festival is organized by Wagner's grandson Wolfgang (*below, center*), who took over the organization of the festival from his mother in 1951. Although Wagner had originally envisioned the theater as a showcase for German music, only his works are performed during the festival today.

A band performing for 85,000 fans at the Sport plätz in Berlin.

JAZZ

In the 1960s, German musicians began experimenting with "free jazz," a form of jazz that began in the United States in the late 1950s. German "free jazz" is characterized by the wild combination of different types of sounds, from contemporary classical music to strange experimental tones. Several German jazz musicians, such as pianist Alexander von Schlippenbach, trombonist Albert Mangelsdorff, trumpeter Manfred Schoof, and saxophone player Gunter Hampel have produced innovative "free jazz" pieces.

The annual jazz festival in Berlin offers a showcase for jazz performers.

POP AND ROCK

German pop and rock bands such as Scorpions, H-Bloxx, Modern Talking, U96 have had international success. Germany's Gregorian chants of the 8th and 9th centuries have made a surprising comeback in the pop charts, adapted by the group Enigma.

MOVIES

Fritz Lang's movie, The Last Will of Dr. Mabuse, *showed a madman speaking Nazi philosophy. This scene attracted the attention of Nazi propaganda chief Joseph Goebbels, who asked Lang to supervise German movies. Lang refused to be associated with the Nazis and left the country that very day, moving to the United States.*

In the 1920s, Fritz Lang was one of the leading names in German cinema, along with Ernst Lubitsch, F.W. Murnau, and G.W. Pabst.

During the Hitler years, creative activity was repressed and film making was used mostly for propaganda purposes. Immediately after the war, with more urgent matters to attend to at hand, the German reconstruction disregarded the role of movies. But in the 1960s, the Young German Film movement, echoing in some ways France's New Wave, took place. Creative individuals such as Alexander Kluge, Volker Schlöndorff, Rainer Werner Fassbinder, and then Werner Herzog, Wim Wenders, and Margarethe von Trotta came into the forefront of the industry.

Successful filmmakers of the 1990s include Soenke Wortmann, who brought the comic book *The Most Desired Man* (1995) to the screen; Helmut Dietl, with his biting social satire *Schtonk!* (1991); Heinrich Breloer, winner of an Emmy award in 2002 for the TV movie *Die Manns*; Doris Dörrie, who has experimented with different genres, such as thrillers (*Happy Birthday*, 1992) and intelligent comedy (*Nobody Loves Me*, 1995); and Detlev Buck, who in *Mens Flophouse* (1995) draws on the dry humor of his Frisian homeland in the entanglements of his laconic heroes.

German film producer Bernd Eichinger now works with an international team that produced Isabel Allende's novel *The House of the Spirits* and *Smilla's Sense of Snow*. German director Wolfgang Petersen has established himself in Hollywood with films such as *The Perfect Storm* (2000).

Film production is generously funded through arrangements with television companies and by a series of film awards. Although German television is not owned by the government, it is controlled by the states. Nevertheless, TV movies such as the epic *Heimat*, a depiction of life in the North German plain, have enjoyed much creative output in recent years.

THEATER

In the 17th and 18th centuries, the individual German kingdoms set up their own state theaters and encouraged and competed for the best playwrights and actors. Today there are over 350 theaters in Germany, 160 of them publicly owned. They receive generous government subsidies so that performances remain affordable for the average member of the public.

German drama started in earnest with the works of Gotthold Lessing (1729–1781), Johann Wolfgang von Goethe (1749–1832), and Friedrich Schiller (1759–1805). Goethe, a voice of the Romantic movement, wrote about the emotional, apolitical individual, with terror lurking just beneath the surface of a peaceful scene. Schiller felt that the theater should have the moral role of instructing the audience, a viewpoint shared by Germans today. In addition to works by these three authors, Shakespearean plays are also perfomed regularly in German theaters.

Monuments in honor of Johann von Goethe, the great German poet and playwright, can be found throughout Germany.

Later German dramatists include Bertolt Brecht (1898–1956) and Peter Weiss (1916–1982), whose play, *Marat/Sade*, was a revolutionary theatrical experiment. Günter Grass's highly political play, *The Plebeians Rehearse the Uprising*, is based on the 1953 uprising in East Germany. Heiner Müller's plays analyze Germany's past and present, while Harald Mueller's *Totenfloss* shows a vision of the world after a nuclear disaster. Modern-day women dramatists in Germany include Gerlind Reinshagen and Friederike Roth.

Open-air theaters spring up throughout Germany during the summer. The Mulheim Theater Days Festival stages new plays each year.

THE PLAYS OF BERTOLT BRECHT

Brecht (1898–1956) was a prolific playwright who developed a unique style of "epic theater." His plays imitated the deeds of humanity through an "alienation device," presenting familiar events and actions in a strange way, but generally avoiding either approval or condemnation of these actions. It was left to the audience to judge the right or wrong of the situations presented, a judgment that Brecht hoped audiences would continue to act on when they left the theater.

He founded a school literary magazine at the age of 15, writing short pieces and his first play in his late teens. His early ideas and beliefs were destroyed by World War I, and his experience of war comes through in *Baal* and *Drums in the Night*. Brecht wrote numerous plays during the 1920s, including *In The Jungle of Cities* and *The Rise and Fall of the City of Mahagonny*, as well as a series of short pieces for small groups of performers without an audience. The most famous play from this period was *The Threepenny Opera*, a satirical depiction of life among beggars.

Two plays written in 1931, when he had become a Marxist, *The Mother* and *Saint Joan of the Stockyards*, were hardly performed at the time because of their highly critical views on the failing Weimar Republic. *Saint Joan* depicted a chilling example of how capitalism could exploit people.

Brecht left Germany in February 1933—the day after a fire destroyed the German parliament and showed the true nature of the Nazi regime— traveling to Denmark, Sweden, Finland, the Soviet Union, and finally the United States. In exile, he developed the theory that the beginning of fascism lies in the economic crisis of capitalism. He produced antifascist plays like *Round Heads and Pointed Heads* (which saw racism as a diversion from the real contest between exploiters and exploited) and *The Resistible Rise of Arturo Ui* (a comical parody of Hitler's rise, showing the links between big business and fascism).

Some famous plays were written during this period: *The Life of Galileo* and *Mother Courage and Her Children*, both warning of Nazism; *The Good Woman of Szechuan* with its Marxist message that the good in every person is destroyed by alienation; and *The Caucasian Chalk Circle*, a complicated play within a play where good ultimately triumphs.

Brecht returned to Berlin in 1948, where he set up a theater ensemble and continued to write, while becoming increasingly unhappy about the culturally repressive East German regime. He died of a heart attack in 1956.

LITERATURE

In German literature, the *Nibelungenlied* poem written around 1200, which tells of the dispersal of the German people, is considered an early literary milestone.

Three centuries later, Martin Luther, the founder of Protestantism, translated the Bible into German at the same time that the printing press was developed by Johannes Gutenberg. These two events greatly contributed to the widening use of written German.

During the 19th century, Theodor Fontane (1819–1898), a popular social novelist, and poet Rainer Maria Rilke (1875–1926), emerged as important literary figures. After the German Empire was founded in 1871, a massive wave of writers focused on German patriotism and nationalism. On the other hand, influential philosopher Friedrich Nietzsche's ideas criticized these values.

After World War I, the Weimar Republic saw the rise of Expressionist writers such as Thomas Mann (1875–1955), whose *Buddenbrooks* and *Death in Venice* were highly successful; Herman Hesse (1877–1962), who won the Nobel Prize in 1946; and Franz Kafka (1883–1924), whose works like *The Trial* and *The Castle* portrayed humanity's powerlessness in life.

Many modern German writers explored the guilt and angst of dealing with their Nazi past. Günter Grass (b.1927) sees the role of a writer as a highly political one. In the 1990s he was one of the few who spoke critically of German reunification. Grass won the Nobel Prize in 1999.

Heinrich Böll (1917–1985) published his *Billiards at Half Past Nine* in 1959—the same year as Grass's famous *The Tin Drum*. Eastern German writer Christa Wolf's (b. 1929) *The Quest for Christa T* describes the conflict between historical development and the protagonist's individual claims.

An illustrated Cranach Bible from the 16th century provides a good example of the old German script.

The famous relief *Adoration of the Kings,* created by Stephan Lochner in the 1440s, adorns the ambulatory of the Cologne cathedral.

FINE ARTS

There are more than 4,500 museums and art galleries throughout Germany. Exhibitions are partly funded by the government, with some sponsorship from large corporations such as BMW.

Albrecht Dürer (1471–1528), in many ways a Renaissance man, was a talented goldsmith, writer, painter, and graphic artist. He is known today mostly for his woodcuts and engravings. Others, such as Hans Holbein the Elder (c.1465–1524) and Hans Holbein the Younger (1497–1543), were successful portrait painters; while Lucas Cranach (c.1472–1553), a friend of Martin Luther, became the official Reformation painter. Caspar David Friedrich (1774–1840) was an outstanding Romantic artist.

The Expressionist movement flourished in the early 20th century until it was banned by the Nazis. Some of the champions of this movement are Ernst Barlach (1870–1938), who showed human suffering in sculptures. Painter Wassily Kandinsky (1866–1944), who lived in Munich and developed an abstract color art, and the Swiss artist Paul Klee (1879–1940), who brought the Cubist movement to Germany, developed the abstract movement in Munich. A leading abstract artist was Max Ernst (1891–1976), whose use of collage techniques and Dadaism helped to start the German Surrealism movement after World War I. His works done from 1936 to 1938 gave his audience a hint of the horrors of Nazism.

More recent artists are Joseph Beuys (1921–1986), who used action art with social and political dimensions; Georg Baselitz (b.1938), known for his upside-down work; Markus Luepertz (b.1941), used motifs inspired by German ideology; Bernd Koberling (b.1938), who derives her themes from nature; and Rebecca Horn (b.1944), famous for sculpture "performances."

ARCHITECTURE

Germany's architecture covers a wide range of beautiful architectural styles, from the gothic-period Cologne cathedral to the expansive baroque designs of Potsdam's Sans Souci Palace and the neoclassical shapes of Berlin's Schauspielhaus. Unfortunately, much of the old, splendid architecture in the former East Germany has been destroyed, not only by Allied bombs during World War II, but by years of neglect, which have led to the demolition of these buildings for safety reasons.

The Bauhaus style was the creation of German architect Walter Gropius and dominated German architectural styles from 1919 to 1933. The Bauhaus style focused on function, uniting engineering and art.

Some outstanding contemporary buildings in today's Germany include the BMW building in Munich; the Stuttgart television tower designed by Fritz Leonhardt; the new Philharmonie in Berlin by Hans Scharoun; and the Gallery of the Twentieth Century by Ludwig Mies van der Rohe.

LEISURE

GERMANS ENJOY A HIGH STANDARD of living in relation to other countries in the world. It used to be common for families to spend their annual holiday period on a Mediterranean beach. However, over the past 10 years, the standard has dropped and, with 4 million unemployed, many families can no longer afford to spend their holidays abroad.

Germans generally have six weeks' paid vacation a year. They spend their leisure time in a variety of ways and belong to several hobby clubs that reflect their interests. Leisure activities in Germany account for about 20 percent of the average person's spending, and leisure has itself become an important industry. The German Leisure Association researches leisure spending and patterns of behavior and gives out information to the public.

Opposite: **German tourists visit the Zugspitze, the tallest mountain in Germany.**

Left: **Two children ride their bicycles along the bicycle path by the Rhine River in Düsseldorf.**

Sailing is a popular sport in Hamburg.

SPORTS

One in three Germans is a member of a sports club and spends a lot of time training in his or her particular sport. Schools benefit from a government funding program that every now and then upgrades their sports facilities, gyms, athletic tracks, and swimming pools.

Gymnastics has been popular since the 19th century and is now funded by the German Sports Aid Foundation, an organization that is supported by private donations and lottery and is not run by the government. Whereas the former East Germany used to invest large sums in training athletes, funding is now scarcer in the unified Germany.

Jogging is popular as a cheap and quick sport for those trying to keep fit. For those who prefer swimming, public pools are found in all big and small cities, including several spa pools and the Olympic Pool in Munich.

Handball, volleyball, squash, basketball, and cycling all remain popular. There is also an interest in Grand Prix racing; a race in the Eifel Mountains near Heidelberg takes place every year.

SOCCER

Soccer is the most popular participatory and spectator sport in Germany. The country has an illustrious soccer tradition. The former West Germany won the World Cup three times—in 1954, 1974, and 1990. It was also runner-up four times, in 1966, 1982, 1986, and 2002.

In 1954, West Germany overcame all odds to beat a Hungarian team that is still considered by many to be the greatest team ever assembled in soccer history.

In 1974, the West German team was beaten by East Germany in an opening round match. It was the only time the two Germanys played each other in a competitive game. But legendary stars Franz Beckenbauer, Gerd Müller, Sepp Maier, and Paul Breitner turned the tide for West Germany, winning the championship by beating the Netherlands.

The 1990 team, which beat Argentina, was coached by Beckenbauer. The German team also won the European Championship in 1972, 1980, and 1996.

Top league clubs like Bayern Munich, Borussia Dortmund, and Bayer Leverkusen take part in European competitions, with Bayern being the most successful. Many current top players have gone to play in the Spanish and Italian leagues, to pit their skills against other top class players.

Most Bundesliga (domestic league) games are played on Saturday afternoons, and television excerpts are shown on Saturday evenings.

After the reunification the former national East and West German teams have merged into one.

German soccer player Miroslav Klose attempts to get the ball past Brazilian defender Cafu in the final game of the 2002 World Cup in Yokohama, Japan. Brazil won the championship with a score of 2–1.

TENNIS

Boris Becker (*below*) and Steffi Graf put German tennis on an international footing, equalling such powerhouses as the United States and Sweden.

Becker turned professional at the age of 15 and won the Wimbledon singles title in 1985 when he was only 17. He won the prestigious competition again the following year. He has also won the U.S. Open and the Australian Open. Graf made a name for herself in the late 1980s, reaching her peak in 1988 when she won the tennis Grand Slam—all of the four top competitions in the world.

In 1989, West Germany beat Sweden in the Davis Cup to become the champion tennis nation. The following year, a West German double effort saw Graf and Becker take the Wimbledon singles titles yet again. Boris Becker won the Wimbledon single title three times and Steffi Graf won it six times. After winning 107 titles during her career, Graf was chosen as one of the best female athletes of the century in a survey conducted by CNN in 1999. In 2001 Steffi Graf married Andre Agassi, a famous American tennis player.

An upcoming star to rival Graf and Becker was Michael Stich. He was the country's youth champion in 1984, and turned professional in 1988 at the age of 20, having completed his schooling and taken the *Abitur* exam. Becker, Graf, and Stich have retired from professional tennis.

German international success in the sport has spurred tennis playing throughout the country, and numerous new tennis clubs have sprung up.

THE GREAT OUTDOORS

Germans love to participate in outdoor activities, which they feel bring them closer to the freedom of the hills and forests. Hiking, walking, and rock climbing, particularly in the mountains of southern Germany, are popular pastimes on weekends and holidays.

The traditional alpine lifestyle of fresh air and healthy food is a real part of German folklore. There are well-marked hiking trails in the Alps, and mountain huts provide food and shelter along the way for people on long hikes. Boy scout trips and outdoor camps in the hills have traditionally been part of the school system. And adventurous mountaineers attempt to scale the Zugspitze or one of the smaller peaks.

Horseback riding is popular, especially in Rhineland-Palatinate, the Neckar valley, and Franconia. Water sports are also popular: boating trips are available on the Mosel and Neckar rivers; sailing and windsurfing are practiced on the North and Baltic Seas and on the Mecklenburg lakes; and canoeing takes place on the Neckar and Lahn rivers and in the Black Forest. In the Bavarian rivers, trout fishing is common. Salmon is found in the Danube. Deep-sea fishing trips can be arranged from Helgoland. Germans must pass a rigorous exam in order to obtain a fishing license.

Vacationers can take the ski lift to the top of the Zugspitze for a spectacular view of the German Alps.

The most popular German card game is skat, which was developed in the early 19th century. Three players use a pack of 32 cards and start bidding. The winning bidder takes on the other two players and has to win more than half the available points in order to win the game.

WINTER SPORTS

Skiing is popular and possible during most winters as there is usually enough snow. The Alps are the main skiing area, and while most of the accessible slopes and facilities are in neighboring Austria, the sport remains extremely popular. The town of Garmisch-Partenkirchen is the skiing center of Germany and is extremely popular as a weekend trip from Munich and other southern cities. Cross-country skiing is popular in the Bavarian and Thuringian forests, along with tobogganing, bobsledding, and curling (a game played on ice in which two teams slide curling stones toward a mark in a circle). Ice skating is another popular sport, especially on the frozen Bavarian lakes and Hamburg's network of waterways.

The country's superb training facilities have helped Germany produce such outstanding winter sports superstars as Katarina Witt, who won numerous championships for the former East Germany, including Olympic gold medals in 1984 and 1988. In the 2002 Winter Olympics at Salt Lake City in the United States, Germany finished on top, with 35 medals.

AT HOME

Reading books, magazines, and the country's many local newspapers are common forms of relaxation, along with watching television. Card games are popular, especially bridge and skat.

Do-it-yourself home improvement is an increasingly popular leisure activity. Growing vegetables and flowers in plots, often on the outskirts of towns, though sometimes near town centers, is another form of relaxation for many apartment occupants. And, of course, the car-loving Germans love to clean, polish, and maintain their vehicles, then drive them to visit friends or explore the countryside.

VACATIONS

The generous amount of annual leave from work, as well as school breaks, allows most Germans to take a family vacation for at least two weeks every year. Germans enjoy traveling and exploring different countries—whether it be the beaches of the Mediterranean from Spain to Greece, or far away places in Asia, Africa, and North America.

Vacationing by the seaside is most popular among Germans, especially for those interested in water sports. Many also enjoy meeting people and sampling the local cuisine of the countries they visit.

Despite the economic slow down, Germans are still some of the world's greatest tourists, traveling mainly to Austria, Italy, Spain and the former Yugoslavia, as well as Greece, France, and Mediterranean resorts. There are package tours that cater especially to German tourists, with German food and beer on sale at resorts such as Rimini in Italy, and Benidorm in Spain.

Travel restrictions imposed on former East Germans proved frustrating for a people who love to travel and see exotic places. This inherent love for travel may have triggered the first steps of the peaceful revolution of 1989. Within Germany, vacations can be spent visiting the Black Forest, Alpine foothills, inland lakes such as Lake Constance (Bodensee), Chiemsee, and Sylt Island near Denmark.

A hotel and winehouse in Assmannshausen, a town in the Rhine valley that produces good red wine. The town also has special springs that some people believe can cure rheumatism.

FESTIVALS

GERMANY DOES NOT CELEBRATE ANY NATIONAL FESTIVALS, not even a national day. Germany does, however, celebrate the reunification of the country on October 3. What it lacks in national festivals, Germany has in regional festivities. Each city and state in Germany celebrates colorful festivals that date back hundreds of years. Many of these festivals have been revived to preserve the local heritage and to boost tourism.

Folk festivals, often with a Christian focus, take place in towns every year, livened up by traditional entertainment and handicraft stalls. Many pre-Christian rituals have survived in these festivals. For instance, the summer solstice of June 24 is linked to the Feast of St. John the Baptist, but the practice of rolling burning wheels, which represent the sun's rays, down hills is not Christian.

Left: **German children make gingerbread houses for Christmas under the careful supervision of their mothers**

Opposite: **The Landshut Wedding festival is held every few years in Bavaria to remember the wedding of Prince Georg von Wittelsbach in 1475. During this festival, which always takes place in the summer, people dress in lavish medieval costumes and parade the streets.**

Masks of all shapes and sizes appear during the carnival in Freiburg.

CARNIVAL

Tied into pre-Christian fertility rites and pagan beliefs, the pre-Lenten carnivals take place mainly in the Catholic areas of Germany. People celebrate by wearing terrifying masks that resemble witches, spirits, and demons, as well as taking part in costume balls and dress competitions.

One of the more famous carnivals takes place in Cologne, where 105 local associations elect three people to dress up as the Carnival Prince, the Peasant, and the Virgin for the duration of the carnival. These characters, usually middle-aged business people, wear costumes and throw toffees at the crowd from their privileged positions in the major parades.

Cologne's carnival starts at precisely 11:11 A.M. on November 11, but gets into full swing during the *Tolle Tage* (TOLL-eh TAHG-eh) or "Crazy Days," just before Lent. The Thursday before Lent is known as Women's Day. On this day women cut off the neckties of any men within reach.

On Sunday a big informal procession takes place. The main procession, called *Rosenmontag* (ROWZ-en MONN-tahg), takes place on Monday. The *Rosenmontag* includes a jester's speech with funny references to local and national politics. Local songs are sung by the large crowd as the processions go by.

Munich's carnival has a young couple, dressed as the *Prinz* (PREENTZ) and *Prinzessin* (preen-TZE-TZIN), prince and princess respectively. They take part in a stylish procession that includes a dance on Shrove Tuesday, in which the women of the fruit and vegetable market perform a dance.

In the town of Elzach in southern Germany's Black Forest, masked "fools" run through the town wearing large decorated hats and hitting people with blown up hogs' bladders. In Rottweil rival groups of "fools" jump through the town's Black Gate at 8 A.M. Meanwhile, jesters' banquets are held in Stockach and Grosselfingen, as well as in Lindau on Lake Constance.

THE MUNICH OKTOBERFEST

Every year since October 12, 1810, there has been a beer drinking festival in Munich. The Oktoberfest began as a horserace held in honor of the marriage of Bavarian Crown Prince Ludwig I and Princess Therese von Sachsen-Hildburghausen of Saxony.

In the following years, the race was combined with the state agricultural fair, and booths serving food and drinks were introduced. By the 20th century these booths had developed into large beer halls.

Today, the Oktoberfest lasts 16 days; it starts in September, as the weather is warmer then, and ends on the first Sunday of October. The festival is internationally famous and attracts tourists from every corner of the world. The central attraction is the huge beer tents where one can drink beer from huge quarter-gallon (1 liter) glasses. After a couple of these, people will jump on the benches and tables and sing traditional drinking songs while waitresses bustle between the long tables bringing additional drinks. Outside the beer tents, there are side shows, a fun fair, trinket stalls, and musical performances as well as a range of traditional food stalls.

During the *Oktoberfest*, the beer tents in Munich are filled with hundreds of people. An estimated 5.9 million people attended the 2002 fest.

119

OTHER DRINKING FESTIVALS

Some regions have their own festivals to celebrate successful harvests. During Stuttgart's *Volksfest* (FOLK-fest), a harvest festival, up to 1.5 million gallons (5.6 million liters) of beer and 300,000 chickens are consumed. The festival has been held each year since 1840. In Erlangen, the *Bergkirchweih* (BAYRG-keersh-vye) festival starts on the Thursday before Pentecost and lasts for 12 days. Beer sampling and brass bands add to the fun.

Various wine festivals are enjoyed in the Rhineland. In November wine makers will place brooms outside their doors as a signal that their wine is ready. They then turn their homes into drinking places for the next couple of months.

CHRISTIAN FESTIVALS

Epiphany on January 6 is a public holiday in the Roman Catholic states. In the countryside, children dress up as the three kings, with the letters C (for Caspar), M (Melchior), or B (Balthasar) sewn into their costumes.

Good Friday is a public holiday, and many Christians fast or do not eat meat for one day. On Easter Sunday children search for the Easter Hare and eat decorated hard-boiled eggs. Easter Monday is the time for egg-rolling competitions.

Ascension Day is a public holiday, where processions and blessing of crops are held. Corpus Christi is celebrated only in Catholic areas, with elaborate altars and flower pictures placed along roads and processions.

The last day of October is the Protestant celebration of Reformation Day. November 1 (All Saints Day) and November 2 (All Souls Day) are times for tidying church graveyards and laying new wreaths. November 10 is St. Martin's Day, when Protestant churches hold celebrations honoring Martin Luther and Catholics honor a saint with the same name.

Christmas celebrations are family affairs. On December 5 children leave shoes outside their rooms to be filled by "Saint Nicholas." Families put an advent wreath on the table and decorate their homes with fir branches, while children open advent calendars every morning from December 1 until December 24, Christmas Eve.

On the fourth Sunday before Christmas Eve, the traditional "Christmas Markets" open in town squares around Germany. Decorations as well as last-minute goodies for family celebrations can be bought there. The most famous one takes place in Nuremberg where the local delicacy is a type of gingerbread called Nuremberg *Lebkuchen* (LEH-p-KOO-hen). A popular drink to be enjoyed in the cold days is *Gluehwein* (GLOO-vine), or mulled wine. The main celebrations take place on Christmas Eve, rather than Christmas Day. The tree is decorated on Christmas Eve, after which many Germans attend a special midnight service in church.

PROCESSIONS

Mounted processions are held during religious celebrations. The *Kötztinger Pfingstritt* (CURTS-tin-ger PFING-stritt) on Whit Monday involves 500 costumed horses and riders riding 4 miles (6.4 km) to an open-air Mass. One festival that remembers the death of Jesus Christ is celebrated with mounted processions in Bad Wurzach and Weingarten. Other celebrations that involve horse riding take place to honor particular Catholic saints.

Catholic children walk down the aisle of a church during their First Communion service.

121

A troubadour (wandering singer) strums his lyre during a medieval festival in Bamberg.

VARIOUS FESTIVALS

In Bleigiessen on New Year's Eve, Germans celebrate a ritual that dates from pre-Christian times: they pour hot lead into cold water and try to look into the future.

Horse festivals are popular in northern Germany. They generally take place around Pentecost and include medieval era contests like jousting. During a festival in Kiel and Dithmarschen, competitors try to stay on a wooden figure turned on an axis called Roland's Riding.

Shooting festivals take place from May to August. The largest of these festivals, held in the city of Hannover in July, lasts 10 days and has over 5,000 competitors. Another such festival, Shepherds' Run, is held annually in August near Stuttgart. There, huge processions and open-air dancing combine with an event where competitors run 150 to 300 yards (137 m to 274 m) barefoot over stubbles. The winner is chosen king of the shepherds.

The *Tanzelfest* (TAHNTZ-ehl-fest) in the Allgäu is one of many medieval celebrations in Germany. It lasts for 10 days and people dressed in historical costumes take part in traditional dances. A re-enactment of the Pied Piper legend is held annually in the town of Hamelin (Hameln in German). Some Germans celebrate Walpurgis Night on April 30; they believe that witches and the devil congregate in the Harz Mountains that night. In autumn, the Rhineland in Flames festival holds firework displays.

Labor Day is celebrated on May 1, and the next-to-last Sunday in November is Remembrance Day.

OBERAMMERGAU PASSION PLAYS

In 1633, an outbreak of the plague wiped out many villages in the Bavarian Alps. As the plague approached the village of Oberammergau, the villagers prayed to God and made a promise to perform a passion play every 10 years if only they were spared. Miraculously, the plague stopped short of the village. In 1634, the Passion Play was staged for the first time. In 1700, it was decided that the play would be performed in years ending in "0"; exceptions were made in 1934, to mark the play's 300th anniversary, and in 1984, to celebrate the play's 350th anniversary.

Since then, every 10 years—the next performance will be in the year 2010—the play is performed by a cast of local amateur actors and actresses and countless extras, from May to September. Thousands of Christians, theatergoers, and tourists flock to this tiny mountain hamlet to watch the two-day-long re-enactment of Christ's life and death on the cross.

Over the years, the play has developed to include passages from the Old Testament in addition to the life of Jesus Christ. In 1970, the script was arranged in such a way as to not place the blame of Christ's death on the Jews. In 2000, the rule of hiring only Christian performers was lifted, and for the first time, non-Christian townspeople were allowed to perform in the play.

The venue of the play is a modern structure that can seat up to 4,800 people. The audience faces an open stage that is reputedly the largest open-air stage in the world. The outside walls of many homes in Oberammergau are decorated with beautiful paintings depicting the death and resurrection of Christ (*above*).

FOOD

GERMANY HAS A RICH VARIETY OF FOOD AND DRINK, much of which is grown or produced at home. A combination of richly spiced meats and salted fish, accompanied by vegetables, and washed down with wine or beer is the typical German's hearty meal.

Because most Germans traditionally worked in the fields, they needed to follow a diet rich in protein. Thus, the country's traditional cuisine revolves around red meat and potatoes. However, there is now an increasing number of vegetarian restaurants throughout the country.

In different regions the same food may come in different styles. A Bavarian dish may be prepared differently in Schleswig-Holstein.

Left: Goods displayed in a Munich wine and cheese store.

Opposite: A delicatessen in a Bavarian town. Sausages are a basic component of the traditional German diet.

A wide variety of freshly baked bread is available throughout Germany.

LOCAL SPECIALTIES

Wurst (VURST), or sausage, is the most prominent item of German cuisine. There are over 200 types of *Wurst*, often made from veal, pork, mustard, spices, and curries. Each region has its own type of sausage, like the Bavarian white sausage *Weisswurst* (VYES-vurst) with parsley and onion or the grilled *chipolata* (chip-oh-LAH-ta).

Blood pudding, poultry cutlets coated with bread-crumbs, cuts of beef and venison, smoked and pickled herring from the North Sea, pickled cabbage or sauer-kraut, a potato salad called *Kartoffelsalat* (kar-TOFF-el-sahl-AHT), spiced red cabbage, and mushrooms are found throughout the country, prepared in different ways.

A rich selection of breads is served in restaurants and bought daily in bakeries. Many love the dark rye Pumpernickel breads.

Wine-producing areas such as Baden-Württemberg, Mosel, Franconia, and Bavaria, are particularly famous for their good food. Local specialties include eel, plum and vegetable soup, and fresh herrings in Hamburg; *Hoppel Poppel* (HOP-pel POP-pel), a potato and ham omelette, in Berlin; suckling pig and roast knuckle of pork in Bavaria; ham eaten with Pumpernickel bread in Westphalia; boiled or breaded fried fish, particularly catfish from the Danube, near Passau; numerous varieties of sausage in Nuremberg; and green herb sauce with pork chops or beef in Frankfurt.

Other favorite foods include Bavarian flour dumplings called *Knoedel* (K-NOO-dell) and Swabian noodles called *Spaetzle* (SHPET-ts-leh), which resemble Italian flat noodles, served with meat or vegetables. Pickled radish from Bavaria is a popular accompaniment to beer.

MEALS

Families have breakfast at around 7 A.M., or even earlier, in order for the children to be at school and adults at work by 8 A.M. The typical German full breakfast includes a variety of breads, sausages, salami, and cold meats, along with cheeses and perhaps some jam for a sweet taste, washed down with coffee, tea, or fruit juice. On a daily basis, however, most families simply have fresh rolls, jam and butter, and coffee or tea.

Lunch, the main meal of the day, is eaten between 11:30 A.M. and 2 P.M., and consists of a cooked meal with vegetables. Working people usually have a hot meal at the office cafeteria or a nearby restaurant, or if pressed by time, some hot pastry filled with cheese or sausages. Most school children have lunch at home after school.

The evening meal is generally quite light. In the south, it may consist of a hot meal of sausage, some potato salad, and soup; in the north, it might be cheese, cold meats, and salad. An early evening meal allows people time to pursue a variety of leisure activities.

EATING OUT

It is easy to find good food in Germany. Restaurants, taverns, and beer gardens offer delicious food. Generally, the menu is displayed on a small blackboard outside at the entrance.

Because of the large number of foreign residents in Germany, Germans can choose from a wide variety of international cuisines, such as Italian, Spanish, Greek, Turkish, and Yugoslav. French food, although expensive, has become very popular among the upper class. There are also many cake shops and fast food restaurants. Budget meals are also available at some butchers' shops and department stores.

An outdoor market in Jena sells fresh fruit and vegetables.

ALCOHOL

Germany produces much of its own wine, generally in the Rhineland area. Eighty percent of German wine is white, of the sweet variety.

Wines are categorized into table wines, quality wines, and prime quality wines, and priced accordingly. There are also young wines—like the *Fruehwein* (FROO-vine) or the *Federweisser* (FAY-der-vye-sser)—and sparkling wines, like *Sekt* (SEKT). Wine is not taxed in Germany.

Beer is not only the Germans' favorite drink, but also a major industry. Germany has over 1,200 breweries, 5,000 different varieties of beer, and is the second largest brewer of beer in the world after the United States.

Germans drink more beer per head—about 33.5 gallons (127 liters) per person in 2001—than any other nation.

A barrel of St. Goarshausen wine.

THE RHEINHEITSGEBOT The German beer industry has been heavily regulated since the 16th century, in order to ensure all beer produced retained a high quality standard. A Bavarian government decree of 1516—the *Rheinheitsgebot* (RHINE-hites-geh-boht), or Purity Law—declared that beer should contain only malt, hops, yeast, barley, water, and nothing else. This standard has been adopted throughout Germany over the centuries as a guarantee of superior taste and quality. Germany also produces a wide range of nonalcoholic beers.

Since Germany is a member of the European Union, beers from other member countries—which many Germans feel are not comparable to German brands as they do not comply with the Purity Law—are now allowed to be sold in the country.

SAUERBRATEN

Literally "sour roast," this hearty dish originated in Rhineland. This recipe serves eight to ten people.

2 ½ pounds (1 kg) beef brisket
4 cups water
1 cup red wine vinegar
2 bay leaves
1 clove
4 peppercorns
2 allspice berries
1 medium-size carrot (peeled and sliced)

1 piece celery root (if available)
1 piece parsley roots (if available)
4 tablespoons oil or margarine
½ cup sour cream
1 ½ tablespoons corn starch
Salt and pepper

Place meat in a deep saucepan. Fill saucepan with mixture of vinegar and water until meat is covered. Add bay leaves, clove, peppercorns, allspice, carrot, celery, and parsley roots. Refrigerate saucepan for 2–3 days, turn the meat over once a day. Heat oil or margarine in a frying pan, brown meat on all sides. Add salt and ½ cup water. Cover pot and simmer for 1 ½ hours on low heat; make sure there is always some liquid, if not, add 1 to 2 tablespoons of water. Remove the meat from the pot, leaving liquid in the pot. Mix sour cream with corn starch (without leaving any lumps) and stir into the pot. Bring mixture to a boil and remove from heat. Add salt and pepper to taste. Cut the meat into serving slices, pour mixture over it, and serve with potato dumplings, or noodles, and boiled vegetables.

BAVARIAN VANILLA CREAM

Simple and delightful dessert from Bavaria. This recipe serves six to eight people.

3 cups milk
1 vanilla pod
4 tablespoons gelatin (unflavored)
$^1/_2$ cup cold water
4 egg yolks
$^1/_2$ cup sugar
1 cup heavy cream (whipped)

Pour milk into a saucepan. Slit vanilla pod, scrape the seeds into the milk, finally adding the pod itself to the milk as well. Leave for 30 minutes. In a saucepan, add gelatin to cold water. Heat water to dissolve gelatin completely. Heat the milk in the saucepan and bring to a boil. Beat egg yolks with sugar until creamy. While beating, slowly add egg yolks into the boiling milk. Remove from heat. While milk is still hot, pour in the dissolved gelatin. Cool until slightly thickened. Slowly stir in the whipped cream. Pour into a fancy mold, or individual parfait glasses. Chill in the refrigerator for at least six hours. Unmold carefully and decorate with fresh fruits, such as berries, mint leaves, and syrup.

*Other options: Bavarian Vanilla Cream can be eaten alone or used as a filling for molded cakes, pies, and cold charlottes. The latter dessert is made by lining the border of a mold with ladyfinger cookies and filling the center up with cream. To make a Bavarian pie, simply add the Bavarian Vanilla Cream to a cooled pie shell or crust and chill in the refrigerator.

MAP OF GERMANY

Aachen A3
Ammersee (lake) C4–C5
Augsburg C4

Baden-Baden B4
Baden-Württemberg B4–B5
Baltic Sea C1–D1
Bamberg C4
Bavaria B3, B4, B5, C3, C4, C5
Bavarian Alps C5
Bavarian Forest C4–D4
Bayreuth C4
Berchtesgaden Alps C5
Berlin C2
Berlin (city) C2
Black Forest B4–B5
Bonn B3
Brandenburg C2, C3, D2, D3
Bremen B2
Bremen (city) B2
Brunswick C2

Chiemsee (lake) C5
Cologne A3

Dachau C4
Danube (river) B5–D4
Dresden D3
Düsseldorf A3

East Frisian Islands A2–B2
Eifel Mountains A3
Eisenach B3
Elbe River C2–D3

Emden B2
Erzgebirge Range C3
Essen B3

Frankfurt B3
Freising C4

Garmisch-Partenkirchen C5

Hamburg B2
Hamburg (city) B2
Hannover B2
Harz Range C3
Heidelberg B4
Helgoland B1
Hesse B3–B4
Hünsruck Mountains A4–B4

Inn River C4–C5
Isar River C4–C5, D5

Jena C3

Karlsruhe B4
Kiel B1
Kiel Bay B1–C1
Koblenz B3

Lahn River B3
Lake Constance B5
Lake Schaal C2
Lausatia (region) D3
Lech River C4–C5, B5
Leipzig C3
Lower Saxony A2, B2–B3, C2–C3
Lüneburger heath B2

Magdeburg C2
Main (river) B4–B3, C3–C4

Mannheim B4
Mecklenburg Bay C1
Mecklenburg-Western Pomerania C1–C2, D1–D2
Mecklenburg (region) C2
Mosel (river) A4, B3
Munich C4
Münster B2

Neckar (river) B4–B5
Neckar Valley B4
Neisse River D2–D3
Nord-Ostsee Canal B1
North Rhine-Westphalia (state) A2–A3, B2–B3
North Sea A1, B1
North Frisian Islands B1
Nuremberg C4

Oberammergau C5
Oder River D2

Passau C4
Potsdam C2

Rhine River B3–B4

Rhineland-Palatinate A3–A4, B3–B4
Ruhr Industrial Area A3
Ruhr River A3, B3

Saarland A4, B4
Saxony C3–D3
Saxony-Anhalt C2–C3
Schleswig-Holstein B1–B2, C1–C2
Solingen B3
Starnbergsee (lake) C5
Straubing C4
Stuttgart B4
Sylt B1

Taunus Mountains B3
Thuringia B3–C3
Titisee Lake B5

Vogelsberg Mountains B3

Weimar C3
Weser (river) B2–B3
Westerwald B3
Wilhelmshaven B2

Zugspitze C5

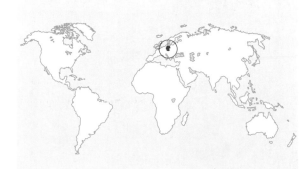

ECONOMIC GERMANY

Manufacturing

- Aircraft
- Chemicals
- Electronics
- Food Products
- Jewelry
- machinery
- Musical Instruments
- Oil Refinery
- Ship Making
- Vehicles

Natural Resources

- Coal
- Fishing
- Natural Gas
- Oil
- Steel and other Metals

Services

- Ports

Agriculture

- Barley
- Potatoes
- Vegetables
- Wheat
- Wine

ABOUT THE ECONOMY

OVERVIEW

Germany is the world's third largest economy and a major industrial and technological power. Due to a lack of significant natural resources, most of the country's wealth is derived from manufacturing and trade. Germany is a leading producer of luxury automobiles, as well as iron, steel, and machinery. Since reunification in 1990, Germany's economy has slowed down due to the burden of absorbing less productive industries and deficient infrastructure from the former communist eastern states. Nevertheless, Germany continues to be the most economically influential country in the EU.

GDP

US$2.1 trillion (2002)

GDP SECTORS

Agriculture 1 percent, industry 31 percent, services 68 percent (2002)

CURRENCY

The euro (EUR) replaced the Deutsche mark (DM) in 2002 at a fixed rate of 1.9558 marks per euro.
1 euro = 100 cents
USD 1 = EUR 87 cents (May 2003)
Notes: 5, 10, 20, 50, 100, 200, 500 euros
Coins: 1, 2, 5, 10, 20, 50 cents; 1, 2, euros

WORKFORCE

41.9 million (2001)

UNEMPLOYMENT RATE

9.8 percent (2002)

AGRICULTURAL PRODUCTS

Barley, cabbage, cattle, fruit, potatoes, pigs, poultry, sugar beets, wheat

INDUSTRIAL PRODUCTS

Cement, chemicals, coal, electronic goods, foodstuff, iron, machinery, shipbuilding, steel, textiles, vehicles

MAJOR EXPORTS

Chemicals, foodstuff, machinery, metals, textiles, vehicles

MAJOR IMPORTS

Chemicals, foodstuff, machinery, metals, textiles, vehicles

MAJOR TRADE PARTNERS

Austria, Belgium, France, Italy, Japan, Netherlands, United Kingdom, the United States

MAJOR PORTS

Berlin, Bremen, Bremerhaven, Cologne, Dresden, Hamburg, Kiel, Magdeburg, Stuttgart

REGIONAL/INTERNATIONAL COOPERATION

European Union (EU), North Atlantic Treaty Organization (NATO), United Nations (UN), World Health Organization (WHO)

CULTURAL GERMANY

Dresden
Modeled after Versailles, the Zwinger was built by Elector Augustus of Saxony in 1719. A collection of Baroque-style buildings, most of these have now been converted into museums. Formal gardens, beautiful fountains adorned with scultpures of mythical figures, and connecting pavilions in the surrounding areas add to the grandeur of the palace.

Cologne Cathedral
A superb example of Gothic architecture, the cathedral was begun in 1248, but completed only in 1880. Its rising towers, detailed sculptures, and impressive stained-glass windows reflect the wealth of the city during the Renaissance and the exquisite local craftsmanship.

Bamberg
Founded in the 10th century, this city's charming architecture retains elements of both Gothic and Romanesque styles. The cathedral, built in Gothic style, and the sculpture of the Bamberg Horseman are two of the city's most important attractions.

Rhine River
Boat rides along romantic castles, vineyards, and picturesque towns are popular among local and foreign tourists.

Black Forest
A favorite holiday spot, the forest is popular with tourists because of its spas; beautiful mountain scenery; large lakes, such as the Titisee; and rivers, where canoeing can be enjoyed. Cities in the forest are also popular for their well-preserved Gothic architecture and cuckoo clock making.

Alps
The Alps of southern Germany on the border with Austria are a favorite winter holiday spot for skiing and snowboarding.

Passion Plays
Every ten years, the town of Oberammergau hosts a series of plays reenacting the last days of Christ's life and his resurrection. Performed by the townspeople for the first time in 1634 as an offering of thanks to God for sparing the town from the plague, the plays are now held in a huge open-air stage.

Neuschwanstein Castle
Built by the eccentric king Louis II of Bavaria in 1886, the fairy tale-like castle was designed by a theater stage decorator. A great admirer of the composer Richard Wagner, the king had the walls of the castle decorated with scenes from Wagner's operas.

Berlin Wall
Built in 1961 by the government of East Berlin to keep its citizens from fleeing to West Berlin, it was opened in 1989 after swift social and political reforms within East Germany. The wall was finally torn down in 1990, but some parts of it have been uprooted are now exhibited in a museum in Berlin.

Rothenburg
The town has managed to retain its 16th century feel, with cobbled streets, quaint old houses, fountains, and charming back alleys. The architecture of its public buildings, such as the town hall, is a mixture of Gothic and Renaissance styles.

Bayreuth Music Festival
Held every year for one month, from July to August, the Richard Wagner festival has been held in the Festspielhaus in Bayreuth since 1882. Only Wagner's operas are performed during the festival.

Nuremberg
The walled Old Town in the city retains much of its Renaissance charm, with its castle, museum, old houses, and fortifications. German artist Albrecht Dürer's house has been preserved as a museum.

ABOUT THE CULTURE

OFFICIAL NAME
Federal Republic of Germany

NATIONAL FLAG
Three horizontal bands: black, red, and gold

NATIONAL ANTHEM
Das Lied Der Deutschen. Text by August Heinrich Hoffmann von Fallersleben, melody by Franz Joseph Haydn originally written for Kaiser Franz II.

CAPITAL
Berlin

STATES
Baden-Württemberg, Bavaria, Berlin, Brandenburg, Bremen, Hamburg, Hesse, Lower Saxony, Mecklenburg-Western Pomerania, North Rhine-Westphalia, Rhineland-Palatinate, Saarland, Saxony, Saxony-Anhalt, Schleswig-Holstein, Thuringia

POPULATION
83.2 million (2002)

OFFICIAL LANGUAGE
German

LITERACY RATE
99 percent

ETHNIC GROUPS (PERCENTAGE)
German 91.5 percent; Turkish 2.4 percent; Greek, Italian, Polish, Russian, Spanish, Serbo-Croatian and other 6.1 percent

RELIGIONS (PERCENTAGE)
Protestant 34 percent, Roman Catholic 34 percent, Muslim 3.7 percent, other or unaffiliated 28.3 percent

IMPORTANT ANNIVERSARY
Reunification of former East and West Germany (October 3)

LEADERS IN THE ARTS
Albrecht Dürer (1471–1528); Johann Sebastian Bach (1685–1750); Georg Händel (1685–1759); Johann Wolfgang von Goethe (1749–1832), Ludwig van Beethoven (1770–1827); Thomas Mann (1875–1955); Hermann Hesse (1877–1962); Walter Gropius (1883–1969); Bertolt Brecht (1898–1956); Günter Grass (born 1927); Werner Herzog (born 1942)

LEADERS IN POLITICS
Konrad Adenauer—chancellor of West Germany 1949–63;
Erich Honecker—leader of East German SED 1971–90
Helmut Kohl—chancellor of West Germany 1982–90; chancellor of reunited Germany 1990 to 1998
Gerhard Schroeder—chancellor of Germany 1998 to present

TIME LINE

IN GERMANY	IN THE WORLD
	753 B.C. Rome is founded.
	116–17 B.C. The Roman Empire reaches its greatest extent, under Emperor Trajan (98-17).
	A.D. 600 Height of Mayan civilization
A.D. 800 Charlemagne crowned emperor in Rome.	
870 Formation of the duchics of Franconia, Saxony, Bavaria, Swabia	
900 Formation of the duchy of Lorraine	**1000**
1138–1254 Hohenstaufen dynasty reigns.	The Chinese perfect gunpowder and begin to use it in warfare.
1235 Emperor Frederick II proclaimed the Peace of Mainz, the first imperial law in German.	
1517 Martin Luther writes the Ninety-five Theses; the Reformation begins.	**1530** Beginning of trans-Atlantic slave trade organized by the Portuguese in Africa.
1555 The Peace of Augsburg	**1558–1603** Reign of Elizabeth I of England
1618 Thirty Years War begins.	**1620** Pilgrims sail the Mayflower to America.
1701 Frederick III of Brandenburg crowns himself king of Prussia.	**1776** U.S. Declaration of Independence
	1789–1799 The French Revolution
1815 Founding of the German Confederation	
	1861 The U.S. Civil War begins.
1862 Otto von Bismarck becomes prime minister of Prussia.	**1869** The Suez Canal is opened.
1871 Founding of the German Empire; Bismarck becomes first chancellor of Germany.	

IN GERMANY	IN THE WORLD
1914	**1914**
Germany joins World War I in the side of Austria.	World War I begins.
1918	
End of the German monarchy; declaration of a republic by the Social Democrats.	
1919	
Paris Peace Conference between France and Great Britain and defeated Germany; Treaty of Versailles signed; election of a national assembly in Weimar	
1923	
Raging inflation; attempted coups by right-wing and left-wing radical groups	
1933	
Adolf Hitler becomes chancellor.	
1939	**1939**
Germany attacks Poland; World War II begins	World War II begins.
1945	**1945**
Hitler commits suicide; Germany surrenders.	The United States drops atomic bombs on Hiroshima and Nagasaki.
1948–49	**1949**
Blockade of West Berlin by the Soviet Union; formation of the Federal Republic of Germany and the German Democratic Republic	The North Atlantic Treaty Organization (NATO) is formed.
1961	**1966–1969**
The government of East Berlin builds the Berlin Wall.	The Chinese Cultural Revolution
	1986
1989	Nuclear power disaster at Chernobyl in Ukraine
Pressure by East Germans for reforms in the government; opening of the Berlin Wall	
1990	**1991**
Unification treaty signed; Chancellor Kohl becomes first chancellor of unified Germany.	Break-up of the Soviet Union
1992	**2001**
Treaty on European Union signed.	Terrorists crash planes in New York, Washington, D.C., and Pennsylvania.
2002	**2003**
The euro becomes Germany's official currency.	War in Iraq

GLOSSARY

Abitur (AH-bee-toor)
Pre-university exam.

Bundesrat (BOON-des-raht)
The federal parliament, comprising nominees from state governments.

Bundestag (BOON-des-tahg)
The federal parliament, elected by citizens.

Cold War
The military and economic rivalry between the capitalist and democratic United States and its allies and the communist and socialist Soviet Union and its allies from 1945 to the late 1980s.

Confirmation
A religious ceremony practiced by Catholics and Protestants in which a youth is accepted as an adult member of the church.

First Communion
A religious ceremony practiced by Roman Catholics in which a child takes consecrated bread and wine, as the body and blood of Christ, for the first time.

Gastarbeiter (GAST-are-byte-er)
Immigrant worker, literally "guest worker."

glasnost
The policy of openly discussing economic and social problems in the Soviet Union that was started by Mikhail Gorbachev in the 1980s.

Grundschule (GROONT-shoo-leh)
Elementary school, which German children start at the age of 6 and lasts from four to five years.

Gymnasium (ghim-NAH-zee-um)
Secondary school that prepares students for the pre-university exam.

Hauptschule (HOWPT-shoo-leh)
Intermediate school that prepares students for admission to a part-time vocational school.

Holy Roman Empire
The empire that was formed from Christian Central European tribes under Charlemagne in A.D. 800., and which lasted until the early 19th century.

Kaiser (KYE-zer)
Emperor of the German empire.

Land (LAHNT)
Individual state within Germany.

Realschule (RAY-ahl-shoo-leh)
Intermediate school that prepares students to a full-time technical school.

synod
A council of church delegates.

xenophobia
The fear and dislike of foreigners and foreign cultures.

FURTHER INFORMATION

BOOKS

Allen, Tony. *The Rhine (Great Rivers of the World)*. New York: World Almanac, 2003.

Epler, Doris M. *The Berlin Wall: How It Rose and Why It Fell*. Wisconsin: Demco Media: 1992.

Lace, William W. *Hitler and the Nazis: World War II (American War Library)*. California: Lucent Books, 2000.

Lord, Richard. *Culture Shock! Germany*. Oregon: Graphic Arts Center Publishing Company, 2003.

O'Neill, Terry (editor). *Readings on All Quiet on the Western Front (The Greenhaven Press Literary Companion to World Literature)*. California: Greenhaven Press, 1999.

Rice Jr., Earle. *The Nuremberg Trials (Famous Trials series)*. California: Lucent Books, 1998.

Roberts, Ian. *Teach Yourself German Language, Life, & Culture*. New York: McGraw-Hill/Contemporary Books, 2000.

Sandford, John (editor). *Encyclopedia of Contemporary German Culture*. New York: Routledge, 2001.

WEBSITES

Berlin Wall. www.wall-berlin.org

Central Intelligence Agency World Factbook (select Germany from the country list). www.cia.gov/cia/publications/factbook

The European Union On-line. http://europa.eu.int/abc/eu_members/germany/index_en.htm

Federal Statistical Office Germany. www.destatis.de/e_home.htm

German Embassy in Washington, D.C. www.german-info.org/relaunch/index.html

German Life (Culture, History, Travel online magazine). www.germanlife.com/about.html

Goethe Institute. www.goethe.de/enindex.htm

Lonely Planet World Guide: Destination Germany. www.lonelyplanet.com/destinations/europe/germany

MUSIC

Beethoven: Symphonien Nos. 5 & 7. Polygram Records, 1996.

Essential Bach. Polygram Records, 2000.

Next Generation (by Gunter Hampel). Birth, 1996.

Twilight of the Gods: the Essential Wagner Collection. Polygram Records, 1998.

VIDEOS

East Germany Opens its Borders. Mpi Home Video, 1990.

Gemany: the Rhine and Mosel, the Romantic Road. Questar Inc., 1997.

Rick Steves Best of Travels in Europe: Germany, Austria & Switzerland. Questar Inc., 2001.

BIBLIOGRAPHY

Bradley, Catherine. *Germany: The Reunification of a Nation.* New York: Gloucester Press, 1991.

Fulbrook, Mary. *A Concise History of Germany.* Cambridge: Cambridge University Press, 1990.

Schnieder, Peter. *The German Comedy: Scenes of Life after the Wall.* New York: Farrar, Straus and Giroux, 1991.

Shlaes, Amity. *Germany: The Empire Within.* New York: Farrar, Straus and Giroux, 1991.

Stern, Susan. *Meet United Germany: Perspectives.* Frankfurt-am-main: Frankfurter Allgemeine Zeitung GmbH Information Services, 1991.

ABC der Hochzeit. www.abc-der-hochzeit.de

Bundesministerium für Familie, Senioren, Frauen und Jugend. www.bmfsfj.de/

Church Office of the Evangelical Church in Germany. www.ekd.de

Deutscher Akademischer Auslands Dienst, www.daad.de

German Galleries. www.germangalleries.com

German Medical Association. www.bundesaerztekammer.de

Kultusminister Konferenz. www.kmk.org

INDEX